MW00929412

Psychic Self Defense
and Protection

Psychic Self Defense and Protection

An Energy Awareness Guide

John Culbertson

Outskirts Press, Inc.
Denver, Colorado

The opinions expressed in this manuscript are solely the opinions of the author and do not represent the opinions or thoughts of the publisher. The author has represented and warranted full ownership and/or legal right to publish all the materials in this book.

Psychic Self Defense and Protection
An Energy Awareness Guide
All Rights Reserved.
Copyright © 2010 John Culbertson
v3.0

Cross Cover Image © 2010 iStockphoto.com/jldeines. Monk Cover Image © 2010 iStockphoto. com/arsenik. All rights reserved. Used with permission. Other Cover Images © 2010 JupiterImages Corporation. All rights reserved - used with permission.

This book may not be reproduced, transmitted, or stored in whole or in part by any means, including graphic, electronic, or mechanical without the express written consent of the publisher except in the case of brief quotations embodied in critical articles and reviews.

Outskirts Press, Inc.
http://www.outskirtspress.com

ISBN: 978-1-4327-5619-2

Library of Congress Control Number: 2010922412

Outskirts Press and the "OP" logo are trademarks belonging to Outskirts Press, Inc.

PRINTED IN THE UNITED STATES OF AMERICA

To my wife, Rose,
You taught me the greatest aspect of protection: that love can truly overcome anything and make all things better. May our love for each other be never ending in our journey through both this physical world and the spiritual one ahead of us.

Contents

Foreword

Protection is basic instinct. Or, more aptly, basic intention. From the beginning we search for that safe place where nothing will harm us. For many of us that spot would be within our parent's arms. When something would go awry we would, by instinct, run to mommy and daddy. How often do you see a shy child seek refuge behind Mommy's skirt? They will, of course, peer around her hip to check out their immediate surroundings but dynamite couldn't budge them from that spot. Why? Because they know, without a shadow of a doubt, that they are protected by that powerful polyester plaid pattern. They know it's safe there. I, for one, found sanctuary behind my grandfather's well-worn recliner. Nothing could get me there. It protected me from everything from thunderstorms to the fiendish Barnabas Collins. Even if my grandfather wasn't in the chair at the time I knew, within my heart, that his essence was enough to take care of me. That faux leather La-Z-Boy was an impenetrable fortress.

Why? Not just because I *believed* it to be. It was because I *knew* it to be. It was my intention to be safe and, by default, I was. Basic and simple.

That's what John has done within this public forum. He has presented a straight forward approach to the essential instinct of personal protection. Basic, simple and natural. It's right in front of us, folks. But every now and then we need someone to flip a brighter light on even the most obvious of things.

Admittedly, I wasn't exactly sure how to go about writing the forward to John's book. Turning it into a shameless self-promo was out of the question since John knows where I live. So I opted to approach it just like John does with this book… by utilizing the clever simplicity of the truth. And the truth is this: John knows his stuff. *(By the way, I'd like to point out that a less-educated sort would tend to use the word "shit" instead of "stuff" at this point. I'm so glad I'm not the kind to stoop to such levels.)* I've seen John in action. He can lock down a space tighter than a jockey holding onto the reins of his steed as he rounds the final curve at the Preakness Stakes at the very moment he realizes that some rube has doused his leather saddle with butter.

John was visiting me when I lived in southern California a few years ago. Being his psychic pimp, I had set him up to read a friend of mine while he was there. (I prefer to not read those I know too well as I don't want my personal feelings to affect the outcome of the session in any way.) My living arrangement at the time was not even remotely conducive to conducting in-person readings (ever live in a milk carton?) so I did what any innovative medium would do: I had John conduct the reading in my car (a rental, no less) while parked in a strip mall parking lot. Once the introductions were made I planned on scurrying off to the nearby Baskin-Robins where I would wallow in an hour-long sugar-induced Utopia (God, I hope my cardiologist isn't reading this).

It was a noticeably blustery day which, for that time of year, was rather unusual in Orange County. Various debris, ranging from leaves and napkins to various sized cups emblazoned with a wide array of recognizable logos, danced across the asphalt to their own inaudible music. John began his process of surrounding the car with Divine Protection. Upon the summoning of the Archangels they then worked together to build, larger and larger, an impenetrable bubble of security all around. The pressure — actually, the term "spiritual weight" would be a better way to describe the sensation — was undeniable. As it strengthened the feeling of the wind upon my face diminished. Bit by bit it faded until it was entirely undetectable. It was as if an unseen grandmother closed a window to prevent her precious doilies from scattering to the floor. It was calm and safe.

Interestingly enough there was one thing that was entirely visible: the dancing debris was still circling around us and the car at full force. The wind still blew. The inanimate ballet troupe continued to perform. Yet I felt nothing. It was as if I was watching a panoramic broadcast of the Weather Channel from the comfort of my own personal biosphere.

Being the professional Doubting Thomas that I am, I stepped a few feet to my left and outside of the protective border John & Company had so efficiently created. Then, and only then, could I once again feel the wind. A cup danced its way toward me, bounced off my foot, spun around and rolled toward the car. Once within the perimeter of protection the cup lost momentum and came to an abrupt halt. I followed the trek of the cup and, once I reached it, I no longer felt the wind. All was calm and peaceful.

And safe.

I looked up at John and asked, "How did you do that?"

He shrugged unassumingly and replied simply, "It's what I do."

And so he does. He not only does it *well*, but he does it *right*. His intent is unfaltering. The knowledge he shares here is vast, and more significantly, it is natural. This innate need is within each of us. It has been from the beginning. Thanks to John we can once again learn to see, and experience, what has been in front of us all along. The light has been turned on for us, folks, so don't just stand there! C'mon in! The light's just fine...

Now, with that being said, who's up for some ice cream?

Charles A. Filius,
America's Extra Large Medium
http://www.extralargemedium.net
Sedona, AZ
January, 2009

Author's Preface — How This Book Came to Be

"Oh God, not another book on psychic self defense!" I grumbled to Marcius, after he prompted me to write the book one evening in 2007. He was already gone, leaving me alone in the room with a white board of information before me.

Marcius is a monk. He's also my life guide. You can always tell when he's around as an almost religious feel pervades the atmosphere. He's a man of few words, but when he does offer them they usually either pack a punch worth of information or they are so incredibly important that it's wise to listen. On the few occasions when I've neglected to listen to what he has told me, I've found myself in a world of turmoil and trouble.

I remember that particular night as though it was yesterday. It will probably always stand out as one of the most important nights in my life.

It was an hour prior to a class that I was slated to teach at the bookstore Starchild, in Port Charlotte, Florida. A store that, later, I would end up buying and owning. The topic I was to instruct others on was psychic protections and energy awareness. At the time, I had no idea I would be writing a book. Instead, I waited impatiently for my students to arrive, eager to share and impart my knowledge to them. The whole time I could feel both Marcius and my protector guide Alexander around me. I could feel the energy in the room grow stronger and stronger. It was as though several spiritual beings were arriving and waiting to attend this class. "This is going to be a good one", I told myself, fully expecting a large crowd to be in attendance. In fact, I was so sure of it that I went and got more chairs, just to make sure enough were available.

An hour later, there I stood, filled with confidence, before the white board. A red marker was in my hand. I was ready to draw diagrams, write important notes, and teach with all the energy that I had not personally felt in a long time.

There was just one problem.

Nobody showed up.

Yep. Not a single person.

To say that I was disappointed would be an understatement. I had felt this whole energy build up, the presence of my guides and other spiritual beings, and was so excited about this class, yet not a single person appeared. Not even the four who had signed up a week in advance!

"I can't believe this! It's times like this that I want to just give up teaching altogether!" I shouted at my guides, watching as the clock approached 7:15.

"Teach the class." Marcius, calm as always, said to me.

This caused me to raise my eyebrows.

"You want me to teach the class with nobody in it?" I asked, feeling somewhat stupid about lecturing to an empty room.

"No, give the lecture to the world."

I stood there, feeling like an idiot, as I dwelt on the instructions from Marcius. I could hear Alexander snickering in the distance. "He won't do it, Marcius, he's too much of a coward", Alexander taunted, but using more colorful language.

So, just to prove my protector guide wrong, I did it. I actually addressed a room filled with no living people other than myself.

In those two hours of teaching, more notes filled the white board than I would ever have thought possible. It was as though information was flowing nonstop, and I could neither talk nor write it down fast enough.

Two hours later, it was over. I stood in wonder at what had just transpired.

"Now, write about it." Those were the last words of the monk that evening, before he disappeared, leaving me in front of a white board with a near perfect book outline - the outline of the book which, along with some additional research and channeled information, you now have and hold in your hands. May it serve you in your metaphysical and spiritual journey, as much as the teaching, researching, and writing of it has served me.

With best wishes for peace profound and always in love and light,

~John Culbertson along with Marcius and Alexander.
Http://www.mysticjohnculbertson.com
- April 30th, 2008

Introduction

There is no doubt in my mind that since you're reading this book you've been going through life, for the most part, dealing with various forms of psychic attacks. Don't be distressed. You certainly aren't alone. In fact, EVERYONE who lives in our physical world will have to deal with some form of a 'psychic attack' at some point in their lifetime. For many of us, especially those of us involved in helping fields such as psychology, counseling, the psychic field, or any field where we are around a lot of people everyday, these attacks will happen at an exceedingly quick rate each and every day of our lives.

It is one of my dreams that those of you who own a copy of this book will be enlightened and informed so that you are better prepared and able to handle these attacks and, more importantly, stay healthy and happy as you move throughout this complex web known as life.

This book has been divided into two sections.

The first section deals with understanding what a psychic attack is.

It is only by fully understanding how energy works that you will be able to understand how psychic attacks happen. Furthermore, it is only after you understand how these psychic attacks happen that you will be in a position to understand how to defend and protect yourself from them.

This is where section two of the book comes in. In this second section we will take a look at various techniques for protecting ourselves, our friends, and even our property from these attacks. As you work with these techniques, you will discover over time that you feel healthier, happier, and more confident in both yourself and where your life is taking you.

With Best Wishes for Peace

John Culbertson

Section I:
Understanding Psychic Attacks

No law or ordinance is mightier than understanding.

—Plato

CHAPTER 1

Understanding John's Belief System

Before I dive into the content of this book it's important that you understand my personal belief system and background.

I was born and raised in Saint Joseph, Missouri. Not a small town by any means, but certainly not a large city. I spent quite a bit of time in Kansas City as a youth and would eventually finish college there with my university degree in psychology.

I was born into a Roman Catholic family. My whole family on my mother's side was, and for the most part still is, Catholic. I grew up being taught prayers of the Catholic Church. I would spend nights reciting the Our Father, Hail Mary, Glory Be, Guardian Angels, and pretty much any other Catholic prayer you can think of.

I loved going to Mass. The ritual of the Mass was one of the most amazing, profound, and beautiful things to my young eyes. When my family couldn't find me they knew of only three places that I could be: my room (for it was my sanctuary), the library (for learning was and still is of prime importance to me), or St. Mary's Catholic Church.

My religion was and still is very important to me. I may not proclaim it like other followers, but deep inside I hold a very high reverence for my born religion. I do say born religion, because I have learned over time that there is truly no right religion. I strongly hold to the belief that every religion is a different path leading to the same outcome and ultimately coming from the same source.

In my youth, it was pretty much a given that I was going to become a Priest. I even went as far as taking the vocational examine and spending some time at a seminary school. Needless to say, that lifestyle was not for me. I found, for all intensive purposes, a better way to serve the divine.

Throughout college I was on a five year quest to discover as much as possible about my religion. A journey that started as a means to explore my own belief system ended up being an adventure through almost every known world religion. This is a journey which I constantly find myself repeating over and over again. Each time I repeat this journey I find that I gain and learn something valuable and new.

You'll find that many of my beliefs tend to be a culmination of various different beliefs. I encourage all my students to listen, research, explore, and most importantly, experiment on their own. What may be right for one may not be so right for another. We are all individuals and as such it is most important that each one of us attempts to discover and find which beliefs work best and make the most sense to us as individuals.

Besides having my born religion, I have adopted several other religious beliefs and lifestyles. Wicca and Positive Thought are among them. Reiki and Shamanism also rank high on my list of beliefs that I follow.

A friend of mine constantly argues that being Catholic and Wiccan is impossible. I know many others in the Wicca community who would agree. After all, Wicca is the idea of renouncing the Christian "God" and following a god and goddess. That is, two parts of a greater whole.

Likewise, I know many Catholic Priest that have basically, in not so many words, said I was doomed for the fires of Hell because I have future visions, can interpret dreams, and at times talk to dead people. The thing is, in each case you have an imperfect human being trying to dictate a perfect divinity's will that neither they nor any other human is fully capable of comprehending while here in this physical world.

The truth is, most of the time I simply smile and nod my head when dealing with others that disagree with my beliefs. Besides, who am I to tell people that what they believe and think is wrong? As long as it's not hurting anyone, I personally can not see the problem with it. Those who do hurt others in the name of any religion, in my book, clearly are misunderstanding their religious beliefs and doctrine.

Historically, we do know that paganism was around long before Christianity was. We also know that most Christians adopted pagan beliefs, changed them, and made them their own. I challenge all people to attend a Wicca or Pagan ceremony and then a Catholic one. See how many similarities you can find. I can promise you, a true Wicca ceremony has the very same holy feel as a Catholic Mass. Wicca, and in fact most pagan religions, are far more loving than many Christians tend to be. Of course, there are also many true Christian followers and believers. When around them, just like with loving pagans, you can feel a sense of compassion and love far above and beyond what has become normal within our world.

You see, it's not the religion that makes a person do good or bad. It's an individuals own free will. It's the reverend/preacher/priest/priestess interpretation of the religion that influences so many people and causes them to obtain inner beliefs which may, at times, lead to acts of hatred, prejudice, and ultimately evil.

I do not bash any religion. I hold them all as being valuable. If others would learn to do the same and, more importantly, learn to act on love alone we would see dramatic changes within our world.

Moving away from my rant, I want to take the time to explain exactly what beliefs I do have. By understanding them you will better understand a large majority of the exercises that we will discuss later in the book.

1. I believe in a higher power.

I don't care if you call this higher power God, the goddess, Father Sky, Divine Will, Architect of the Universe, Cosmic Consciousness, or any other name. I believe it is there and that we are in no position to be able to fully comprehend and understand it. You will see me refer to it as God or god force throughout the text of this book.

2. I believe in angels.

I do not believe that human beings, upon death, become an angel. I do believe that angels are an entirely separate race/breed from the human form. I believe that the vast majority of angels never had nor ever will have human form. I believe that they assist this greater cosmic power known as the god force. I do not believe they intervene into the lives of humans unless humans request them to do so or unless imminent death is at hand prior to a human's time to leave this physical world. I do believe that some may choose to take human form in order to connect, help, or communicate better with us.

3. I believe in spirit guides.

I believe that guides are spiritual beings not existing in our physical world, but in the non physical world. I believe they have different purposes. I think some aid in keeping us safe and healthy and others aid in advising us along our human path. I do not believe they are all knowing. I believe they are in a partnership with us. Just as they seek to aid and help us in certain areas of life, they too at times learn from us and by the things that are happening to us within the physical world.

I can honestly say that I did not have the best childhood in the world. In fact, it was what many would consider to be traumatic. I'll go much deeper into that in my future biography. There were few things that I had available to me to help me get through those rough and horrible times. The things that did aid me were my belief in a higher power and my connection to my imaginary friends. Those imaginary friends, I would later learn, were my guides. The relationship I built with them, I can assure you, was and still is very real. I have learned much from my connection to and with them and I know that my guides have gained a lot from working with me.

I also spent much of my most painful times communicating with various angels. These communications and connections were woven into my being at a young age and were something I, thankfully, never lost. Every time I said a prayer which was about an angel it was as though the angels themselves were present. They too were as real to me as this book is to the reader holding it.

4. I believe that all people are born into this world with a high degree of energy sensitivity.

I have learned that many children tend to shut their sensitivity, and psychic abilities, down over time. This is usually due to non supportive parents and peers that have already been taught/programmed that their sensitivity and abilities either aren't real or aren't important.

When a child gets scolded or punished over and over again for telling people what they see/experience, they eventually will either stop telling the truth, keep those experiences to themselves (like I did), or they will shut down completely, refusing to allow themselves to ever believe in such things again. As you'll discover later, when a person creates or has woven into them a particular belief system, that belief system tends to shape the whole world as they know it.

I would later spend a great deal of time studying both angels and guides. I have heard numerous opinions from many belief systems and the ones which I've chosen to personally believe I have done so because they seem most accurate to me. There will also likely be a future book about angels and guides.

5. I believe in fantasy creatures known as elementals.

An elemental is a creature that most of us commonly think of as being myth or fantasy. Examples of elementals include Elves, Dwarves, Dragons, Gnomes, and Fairies. I believe they exist in the non physical world. I believe that many can come and go from our physical plane, but the majority of people, due to society conditioning, have decided so strongly that they aren't real that they fail to see them.

I believe that, for the most part, these fantastic creatures live their own lives in their own reality. I do think it is possible for them to cross into our reality and us into theirs. I do not, however, think that it's always wise to do so. Still, there is always an exception to every rule. You will see me reference these creatures a few times in this book. I do so because I believe there are times when their aid and help can be beneficial to us and vice versa.

6. I believe that our mind is the most important thing that we have available to us. That through learning to use and control the mind it is possible for anything to happen.

7. I believe in magick equally as much as I believe in prayer.

I believe they are one in the same. I believe that they are two different ways of expressing the same energy. In fact, many times I will perform a magick ritual and then add Roman Catholic Prayers at the end. Why? Because they both act to strengthen the subconscious aspects of the mind, which ultimately leads to reality around us changing form and shape.

8. I believe that love is the most important energy in the world.

With the power of love one is truly capable of obtaining and having anything. I believe we live in a world where we do not understand what love really is. For most people love is possessive. It is very much similar to an "I own you" feeling. True unconditional love goes beyond that possessiveness. It's about connecting at a much deeper level and has nothing to do with eroticism or romantic love.

9. I believe people choose to use energy in a negative or positive way.

I do not think that energy itself is negative (bad). When you see me reference negative energy in this book, know that I'm speaking of how it's being used and not the nature of the energy itself. For all intensive purposes, a person can take energy that is being used negatively and turn it into something positive.

By this time you will have decided if you're still interested in hearing what I have to say about energy and psychic self defense. Some of you will feel that our belief systems clash too much and will want to put this book down and migrate elsewhere to get the information you are seeking.

Others, though not necessarily agreeing with everything they've read thus far, will at least be curious to see what else I have to say.

Still, the rest of you will be smiling, happy and comforted to have found an individual with beliefs finally similar to your own. You will be overjoyed that a person of Catholic origins can combine aspects of their faith with aspects of the new age, new thought, and pagan worlds.

No matter which, you've now had the chance to hear about my own personal beliefs. I'm not asking that you agree with them, I'm simply sharing them with you so you have a better context upon which to understand the rest of this book.

CHAPTER 2

Auras and Psychic Attacks

ALL living beings have an aura. You, me, the plant in the garden…. ALL living things.

Just what is an aura? According to Wikipedia, "An **aura** is a field of subtle, luminous radiation supposedly surrounding a person or object." The belief of many in the new age field is that the aura is the field of energy that surrounds every person and living thing.

The main purpose of the aura is to contain your life force energy. It serves the purpose of protecting you by not allowing your life force energy to dissipate or be drained.

The best way to think of an aura is to think of an egg. Yes, that's right, an egg. Go get an egg right now. Hold it up and look at it. That outside shell of the egg, that's the aura. The inside of the egg is where the human body would be. All of us have this egg-like shell around us. Its purpose is to protect and energize us.

Have you ever felt nervous upon first meeting someone? Have you felt the need to back away when someone walked into your space? In both of these cases you are experiencing one aura making contact with another aura.

When your aura is healthy, strong, and without holes, you usually feel upbeat, happy and energetic and you tend to be in good health. When the aura is weak or has holes you tend to feel down, depressed, tired, sluggish, and your health may be waning.

Those of you who are reading this and are feeling low or excessively tired, I can almost guarantee that your aura is in a weakened state or has holes.

We all know that inside of this egg is the egg white and that this white is a substance that is being held in by the shell. The same concept is true when we talk about our own aura shell. Within our aura is a pool of energy that animates us and makes us alive and vibrant. If we were to poke a hole in the egg shell then the white would ooze out. It wouldn't matter how big the hole was, there would still be some type of leakage that would occur. The same happens when a hole is placed within our own aura. Our energy oozes out.

Of course we don't have people jabbing forks into us to make holes in our aura shell. Even so, we can still get holes in our aura and people can penetrate it. That typically happens in one of two ways.

First, anytime we feel a sense of fear, holes are produced within that aura shell.

When we become afraid or have any variation of the fear emotion (such as sadness, anger, etc) the aura weakens considerably. It is in this weakened state that other people can eventually poke holes in the aura or penetrate the aura. Now, please keep in mind that we are talking on an energy level here. Unless you've developed the psychic ability of clairvoyance (which means clear seeing), it is unlikely that you'll see the aura or holes within it with just the naked eye. Energetically speaking, it does happen. The moment a hole is energetically made within the aura, our energy will start to ooze out. Some people, known as energy vampires, take advantage of these holes by 'sucking' our energy from us. They are literally replacing their own energy, or lack of, with the energy from the aura hole.

Why would someone want to suck your energy from you? The reason people constantly try to suck energy from each other or even battle over the control of each other's energy is because they are lacking in their own energy and they have not learned effective ways of naturally restoring it. Instead of looking for natural ways to restore their own energy, they attempt to take/steal other people's energy. This almost always happens on an unconscious level. We call these people who do this unintentional energy sucking 'energy vampires.'

EVERYONE has been an energy vampire at some point of time in their life and, because of the flawed nature of humans, we will most likely do it again. You, me, and even great spiritual leaders have been or will be guilty of it.

One of the things that we are hoping to do in this book is show you how to naturally restore your own energy so you don't have to steal or get it from other people. The other thing we are going to do is make you aware of how energy attacks happen, so that you can learn techniques to prevent your own energy from being stolen.

The second way we get holes in our aura is by allowing other people to penetrate it. This can be just as harmful as someone producing a fear based emotion within us and taking our energy. Yet, it is almost even more dangerous and common. After all, who amongst us has never had a friend who was in an emotional state and we opened ourselves wide to them, with the hope of making them feel better? The moment we open ourselves, make that heart-to-heart connection, we are giving them a free rein to take and use our energy. Obviously, the most intense example of this is through any type of sexual interaction with another person. That's certainly not the only way. It can also be as simple as a friend in need making a phone call and you opening yourself up to listen to them and their problems.

Keep in mind that we aren't saying that choosing to give your energy to other people is a bad thing. It is, however, your responsibility to know how much you can give without being drained yourself, and to NOT steal or take someone else's energy if yours becomes depleted. Most of us are compassionate people who desire to help those around us. Again, this is all right, as long as you know your own boundaries, and aren't allowing yourself to be drained completely or, worse yet, used.

In the psychological world, the word for the aura is personal boundaries. By having healthy and mature personal boundaries, we are in effect creating a strong aura around us.

Realize that every human problem centers on and around control in some capacity or another. There are some things which we can control and some things which we cannot control. Those things which we are capable of controlling lie within our own aura or inside our own personal boundaries. The things which we aren't capable of controlling are those things which reside outside our aura or personal boundaries.

In order to help keep the aura healthy, it becomes important to let go of and not focus on the things which we cannot control. For example, we cannot control the actions of our romantic partner, yet how many of us try to do so? What we can control is our response to how our romantic partner behaves. Our responses are within our own aura/personal boundaries. The actions of our partner certainly lie outside of our own aura/personal boundaries.

Understand that when we spend energy on things which we cannot control, we end up going through what is more commonly known as suffering. Suffering is the state of agonizing over those things which we cannot control. Suffering, is when we have exhausted our energy and feel that we have none left, and yet keep trying to use energy we don't have available to us.

We always have the choice to say 'no' to things. We have the choice to not suffer and to not be under stress. We have to exercise this choice though and make good use of it.

We've already talked about some of the ways in which you can tell when you have holes in your aura. There are others too. Consider this....

- When you aren't able to say 'no' to something you really don't want to do, there is a hole in the aura and you're being controlled through it.
- When you hear the word 'no' from another person and you aren't able to adapt to that situation, you have a hole in your aura.
- When you don't acknowledge obvious self/personal problems there is a hole in your aura.
- When you find yourself getting upset easily, under a lot of anxiety, or are constantly feeling tired or sensitive, there is a hole in your aura.
- When you experience fear, anger, sadness, stress, anxiety, or pain, there is a hole in your aura.

In all of these cases what we need to do is take the time to regain our own energy and repair the holes that are already within the aura structure.

There are various techniques to seeing and feeling the aura. Techniques anyone can learn or, rather, relearn. I say relearn, because as children most of us had within us these inborn abilities to see and feel auras. For the majority of people who take psychic development classes, they are working on learning to reopen what is naturally already there.

The reason you would want to learn, or relearn, how to see and feel energy, especially the aura, is because by doing so you are giving yourself further tools that will help you to understand how energy attacks, or the loss of energy, happens. When you can see it happening, or even recognize and feel it happening, you will have won over half the battle in the psychic/energy warfare that is happening constantly around us every day of our existence.

Now that we are armed with the knowledge of what the human aura is, let us dive a little deeper into the subject by focusing on a typical day in the life of a typical family.

The Story of a Family

I want you to imagine, if you will, a young couple: Bill and Mary. Bill and Mary are a regular normal family. Bill works for a big corporate company and Mary is a stay-at-home mom who spends the majority of her time raising their son Nathan, who is six.

One morning, as Bill is making his daily commute to work, he gets stuck in a traffic jam. Now, for those readers out there who happen to live in large cities and know exactly what a traffic jam feels like, it's not usually a very comfortable experience. People becoming irritable and impatient, with horns honking and fear building as many people realize they are going to be late for work. Bill feels all this energy, but he doesn't consciously realize he's feeling it. Most of us "normal" people don't.

Eventually that traffic jam lets up and Bill makes it to work. He enters the office and hasn't walked more than a few steps when his boss grabs him and tells him he wants to see him in his office.

In that office Bill gets blasted by his Boss for being late. Of course, what Bill doesn't know is that his boss has just been reamed by his own superior. Blasted by a burst of anger and the fear of being fired, Bill goes back to his stressful job, now feeling weak and tired.

Eventually Bill gets home. When he arrives at home he is greeted by his lovely wife. Not more than a few moments go by before the two get into an argument, started by Bill. Bill storms off to his room to take a nap and Mary is left feeling upset.

Since Mary is like the average woman, we can assume that one of the first things she does is reach for her phone. She calls her best friend, Betty. She just knows that Betty can help her feel better.

Betty has been having an awesome day! So when the phone rings and she sees on the caller ID that it's Mary, she very excitedly picks up the phone. Immediately Mary launches into how badly Bill treated her upon coming home. Betty, being the good friend and kind hearted soul that she is, listens with a great deal of compassion. A good hour goes by, most of it with Mary complaining about how her relationship with Bill is deteriorating. When they hang up, Mary feels great! So great, in fact, that she goes and plays with their son Nathan, who's been feeling very grumpy because he got picked on at school. As they play, Mary begins to feel tired and Nathan begins to feel much better. This family will eventually eat dinner, and then prepare for bed, hoping that tomorrow will bring in a new day and one that won't be nearly as stressful as the one they endured.

Meanwhile, Betty, after getting off the phone with Mary, is feeling very tired now. In fact, she's way too tired to cook. By the time her husband Tim comes home, there is no dinner ready. Tim, after a great day, doesn't really care that Betty hasn't had time to fix dinner and instead suggests that the two of them go out. They go out and enjoy a wonderful meal, and come home and have a nice night of lovemaking. After they finish making love, Betty feels absolutely wonderful, but Tim isn't feeling so hot. In fact, he feels so antsy that he doesn't fall asleep for another three hours and by the time the next day comes around he's feeling like crap.....

Welcome to our world. How many of you have had just one of those experiences above? How many of you have had more than one? I wouldn't be surprised if you were able to identify with at least one of the characters. Be aware, though, that every character in the above story was a recipient of a psychic attack in some form or another.

"But wait!" you say, "I didn't read anything about anyone launching psychic missiles at someone or putting a curse on someone!" Of course you didn't! Because MOST psychic attacks that happen in our world are unconscious and unintentional.

See, when we speak of psychic self defense, what we are really talking about and speaking of is energy awareness. How other people use their energy, how we use our energy, and how to make the most of it without harming or hurting ourselves or others in the process. Sure, we'll get to the darker aspects of the psychic world later, but for now, you just have to realize and understand that what we are primarily dealing with is energy and how people abuse it.

Let's analyze the above story minutely and pinpoint where every single psychic attack happens and why it happens and the reason for calling it a psychic attack.

A Review of the Story

The first attack happens at the traffic jam. Even though people aren't directing their anger at anyone, that angry energy is still bouncing around. Anyone who is sitting there afraid of being late is going to be hit by that angry energy. Remember, fear is the number one culprit when it comes to why other people's energy affects us and why we end up losing our own energy.

When Bill's boss grabs him and tells him he wants to see him in his office, we are dealing with another fear factor. Anyone who has been suddenly summoned to their superior's office usually feels a sense of dread. How his boss did it and how Bill was feeling would determine just how weak the aura was at the time when Bill entered the office. Even if his boss was nice about it, but because Bill had just been caught in the traffic jam and was losing energy in it, we can already assume that Bill is at a below average aura strength.

In that office Bill gets blasted by his Boss for being late. When I use the word 'blasted' what I mean to represent is a literal unleashing of pent up frustration from an event that happened earlier in the day. Most blasts are directed at people who either naturally fear us or who we are close to. Through blasting others with energy we release that energy, no longer feeling the need to carry it with us. This clears our system. What it doesn't do is clear someone else's energy field. All that energy is now within the energy field of the person who was blasted. Thus we have transference of energy going on from one person to another.

While this is certainly one way to get rid of 'negative' vibes, it usually doesn't help others when we blast. Remember, the aura of a person weakens when there is a sense of fear. It's like taking a force field from a sci-fi movie that is at 100% and having it reduced to 50% or less. When the aura is reduced low enough, a blast penetrates right through it and shakes a person at their very core. In fact, it would be like taking a fork and jabbing it through the egg, producing several holes or enlarging a hole that was already there. This scatters the energy of the person who was blasted and will also cause the energy to leak out.

When Bill gets home he gets into an argument with his wife. Of course they get into an argument! Bill has had a work day from the very start that has weakened and torn down his aura and zapped him of his energy all at the same time. He needs energy! Nice as his wife is, she's no doubt opening herself up already on an emotional level when he reaches home. When Bill doesn't feel that's enough or that he's not getting enough energy he will start a fight, as this will allow him to have a more easy access to that energy. When he's had enough or when the two are butting heads with each other because they are battling over each other's energy, he storms away either because he does not want to risk losing any more of his energy OR he storms away because he's gotten what he wants.

Mary calls her friend Betty, because Mary now needs energy! What are friends for? Betty is the typical good-hearted friend. She listens attentively to what Mary is saying because she cares deeply for Mary. Betty begins by asking Mary what happened. The energies of the two women, even from a distance, get linked to each other and the transference of energy from Betty to Mary begins. Mary helps this process by constantly pulling at Betty, asking her questions to put her on the spot and catch her off guard. After all, it's not Betty's responsibility to fix the relationship. Betty doesn't feel that she can tell this to Mary, after all, she is a good friend. So instead of interrupting her, Betty allows Mary to download on her.

This is another important concept. A download is when one person opens their energy field or aura to another, usually out of kindness or compassion, and that person abuses the right by continuously taking more energy and replacing it with their 'negative vibes' that they are carrying around. A blast, in essence, can be a very intense form of a download, but doesn't always have to be a download. Downloading on a friend isn't nice, even if they do allow it to happen. To share and get a little energy out of it is one thing; provided your friends are willing to give the energy and you're not stealing it. To totally monopolize the energy connection is something else all together.

There's another important concept here that's also interesting to note. We don't have to be in direct eye contact with another person for our auras and energy to be affected by each other. All we have to do is form some type of link to that person, such as emotionally via phone. Once any type of link is established with another person you can be assured that the auras and energies are affecting each other.

After Betty gets off the phone she basically feels like crap. Of course Betty feels like crap. She's just had most, if not all, of her energy depleted and replaced with energy she doesn't need in her energy field. Tim does the first right thing in this entire scenario - instead of blasting or allowing Betty to download he simply redirects the energy and offers to go out instead. This is excellent! Unlike Mary and Bill the two are now not competing for energy, but rather are sharing it by doing something they both enjoy together. If there is a mistake that Tim makes, it would be engaging in the process of making love when Betty isn't in an emotionally good state of mind. The very act of making love is the act of an energy exchange. If Betty hadn't been constantly thinking of Mary throughout the evening, then both parties would have probably enjoyed the energy exchange to its fullest. Instead, Betty ends up being filled with the majority of Tim's positive uplifting energy, making her feel great, and Tim ends up freely giving it and taking on the emotional concerns that Betty has had.

So what we are learning here is to be aware that every interaction we have with someone else is an interaction that is based on and around energy. We are either giving energy freely or we are having our energy taken from us. We are either helping another person with our energy, or we are having an adverse effect on them. Likewise, other people either energetically help us or they have a negative impact upon us. This is especially true when we aren't aware of what's happening.

A good exercise for you to do would be to start keeping a journal of your daily interactions with others. Don't just write down what happens and how it happens, go back later and look at it from an energy point of view. Try to really grasp and understand the energy dynamics that are going on in your day to day life. Do it for family members and friends as well. When you start looking at the world from this concept and through the eyes of energy, it takes on a totally different meaning.

After you've done that exercise come back to this book and read on to discover ways of replacing your energy and repairing your aura. These are techniques that DON'T require you to take or compete with someone else for their energy.

CHAPTER 3

Repairing a Weak Aura and Rebuilding Lost Energy

So far we have been talking about the aura and understanding that when it becomes weak it's easy for others to break or crack it and thus have access to the energy within. We've also looked at the concept that we can actively allow other people to freely have access to our inner energy. Finally, we've made it clear that energy dumping, downloading, and blasting is not nice and is not beneficial in any way to either party.

"John, if I can't get energy from other people, then where do I get it from?"

There are basically three ways to restore lost energy that do not involve stealing or taking it from someone else.

1. Sleep

That's right, sleep. Sleep is one of the best and most effective ways of restoring your energy. Not only does getting proper rest restore our energy, but it also aids in mending any holes or cracks that are within the aura field.

How? It's simple. When we sleep it is as though we are driving into an auto repair shop and leaving the car there for a few hours. The car being our body and the energy field connected to it. Our soul takes a leave of absence, journeying into the astral plane. While in the astral plane, guides, angels, and the natural energy of the universe work together to help restore energy and mend the aura shell.

What's the astral plane?

Besides our physical world, the physical plane, there also exists various other planes or worlds. Mostly, they overlap each other. Thus, we have our physical world. We have the emotional world which is overlapping the physical. We have the mental world, which overlaps the emotional. We also have the intuitive which overlaps the mental. Overlapping the intuitive is the spiritual world. When we are active on the physical plane, we are also equally active on the other planes. We can also exist in the other planes without existing in the physical.

The emotional plane we call or deem the lower astral. The mental and intuitive is the upper astral. Beyond that, going into the spiritual planes and beyond are even 'higher' planes.

When we say higher we aren't implying that they are stacked one on top of the other as in building blocks. Rather, they resonate at a higher vibratory frequency.

When we sleep our soul leaves the physical plane. That is the plane where our physical body resides. In fact, it usually moves beyond the mental and intuitive planes as well. While hanging out in the spiritual, the aura on each of the other planes has a chance to mend and repair, and our energy, gets restored and replenished. It is also during this sleep state that our physical bodies repair themselves too.

How much is the proper amount? Only you know that. Some people require much less sleep than others. Regardless of the optimum amount, in order to get good sleep you must take the time to relax before going to bed.

The author has found that the best way to do this is to do some type of relaxing activity (bath, watching comedies on TV, reading a good book) uninterrupted for about two hours prior to sleep. This means that the author typically won't even answer his phone for two hours prior to going off to bed.

You see, all it takes is one family member or friend downloading negative details of how horrible their day has been and how awful the world around us is, to psychically link in and attach themselves to you. How uncomfortable it is to try to go to sleep with someone else's energy bouncing around you! If you must take such phone calls, please use the cutting psychic links exercise that is presented later in this book. Make sure you are clear prior to bed and make sure you go to bed with beautiful and/or positive thoughts and feelings; otherwise you will be doing yourself a great disservice and you'll be drawing to you those things which you don't want or need in your life. We'll discuss more on this in a few moments.

2. **The second way to go about getting energy from the universe and repairing your own aura is through the process of meditation.**

Understand that there are many types and kinds of meditations. When people normally think of meditation they think of long hours of sitting cross legged alone or with some chanting or humming. While this stereotype holds some truth, it isn't all true.

There are two types of meditation that you, the reader of this book, need to focus upon. The first is a standard Prana breathing meditation. The second is a Chakra meditation. As a brief introduction, here are a few things to keep in mind as you go about preparing yourself for meditation.

- Meditation requires relaxation in order to actually be most effective. Like sleeping, it requires some degree of relaxation to have already happened within your body.
- Meditation works best when it's done at the same time in the same place, daily, over a period of time. As you work with the same location and same time you are doing two things. First, you are building up a certain type of energy, a meditation energy, which will allow you over time to enter more quickly into a meditative state. Second, psychologically speaking, by doing it in the same place at the same time over a period of time you are building within yourself a very healthy habit that will aid you for many years to come.
- Meditation requires you to have uninterrupted time alone. This means no kids, no parents, no spouse, no work, no phone calls, no TV, no radio.... uninterrupted time. This is YOUR time. Meditating with a spouse or group is fine and in fact can be very helpful, but the majority of you reading this will want to have 'private time' for your meditation.
- Meditation is best done sitting upright and not lying down. Typically when you try to meditate lying down you end up sleeping and as such defeat the very purpose of meditation altogether. The straighter your spine, the better off you are. Energy will be traveling up that spine, and if it's straight it gives it a more natural path to follow. You do not, however, have to be uncomfortable! In fact, if you're feeling uncomfortable with how you are sitting you won't be able to get the benefits of a good meditation.

- It's best not to cross anything while meditating. When you cross your arms or legs, or even your ankles, you end up closing off energy circuits within the human body. We will be discussing this more a little bit later when we start to get to the techniques of defense.

Now, that I've advised you on what you need to do in order to be able to meditate, you will also want to know about the benefits of meditation. Well, in addition to what I've previously written (the fact that it helps to repair the aura and restore energy), meditation will also give you the added health benefits of lowering your blood pressure and expanding the lungs. Additionally, it provides you with the tools needed in order to be able to still and clear the mind, which can serve so many different purposes in your daily life. Not to mention, it's only through meditation that one learns to separate self from non-self. This is the reason most of us psychics are able to do psychic readings and tell when our guides are talking to us. We've learned to make meditation our friend, and if you work with it I can promise you that it will be a friend well worth having.

So just what do you do to meditate? What are the steps?

For Pranic meditation the basic step is to get up and get into your space as described above, and then focus on your breathing. In the metaphysical world there are three basic breathing patterns that we utilize. These three types of patterns are called deep positive breathing, deep negative breathing, and deep neutral breathing. When we say negative breathing we don't mean 'bad' breathing. We simply mean a more yang type of breathing that activates the yang energy within.

In the Eastern traditions there are two types of energies. Yin energy is calm and relaxing. It's a more feminine type of energy. Yang (pronounced yawn) energy, on the other hand, is more active and fast. It tends to be more of a masculine type of energy.

Positive breathing activates the Yin energy within. Negative breathing actives the yang energy.

For the purposes of this book we are going to focus on deep neutral breathing.

To do deep neutral breathing you begin by deeply inhaling air through the nose. As you inhale, mentally count to six. Once you reach six, you should hold your breath for a count of three. Now, exhale through the mouth while mentally counting to six again. Finally, you hold your breath again for a count of three. Continue this pattern. The idea is to get to a point where your mind gets in tune with the pattern so that you no longer have to count, but rather let the breath do its own work. It is at this stage, when you can focus on nothingness, and simply follow the breath that you will be meditating in a very effective way.

A few notes about this exercise needs to be stressed. First, if you have any type of existing medical condition or if you happen to be pregnant, it would be a good idea to get your doctors permission before performing this particular type of meditation. Additionally, it would be advisable not to perform this particular type of meditation while driving or operating any type of heavy machinery.

Now, there is no doubt that while you attempt this, especially if you aren't use to meditating, you will be thinking anywhere from a few to several thoughts that pop into your head. Thoughts ranging from "Is this working?" to "Did I put the milk away?". Just let all of these thoughts come into the mind and then slowly push them out. Do not attempt to analyze them, do not attempt to hang on to them or remember them, and for goodness sake, don't beat yourself up for having them.

At first the mind will be like a young child who constantly wants to get into mischief because of its curious nature. As a parent your job is to redirect it back to its original purpose. In this case, that original purpose is the purpose of focusing on nothingness and following the breathing pattern. Over time, fewer thoughts end up coming in and you wind up having a greater deal of control over your mind.

It is in this meditation state, when you are in that alpha state, that the energy begins to recuperate and the aura begins to mend. You can help in this process, but to do so you need to understand another concept.

Many people in the new age field talk about something called the white light and the polar opposite of it which is blackness. When a person speaks of white light energy they are talking about imagining or visualizing a source of divine energy. There are many ways to do this. The most common way to picture the white light energy around you is by imagining that you're taking a shower. As the warm water starts to fall down and around you it starts to turn into a stream of white light. Soon you see that whiteness totally enveloping your body and the area around you.

Another very popular way of getting into the white light energy is to imagine walking into a light bulb that is turned off. Seeing the glass around you and pretending that you are standing in the center of the light bulb. Suddenly and without warning someone turns the bulb on and you find yourself being flooded with brightness.

There are many other ways to surround yourself with white light energy, but these are the two most common and the two that would be recommended to you to try first.

Once you understand how to put yourself into this white light energy, you can meditate, allow yourself to enter that alpha state, and then focus on that white light energy being not only around, but inside of you. This energy will help to repair your aura.

You can also, when you feel that your aura is in a weakened state, visualize or imagine that there is a lot of dirt or blackness around you. By pretending that you are pushing all that away from you and into mother earth beneath you, you will also be aiding the aura in its recovery and healing process.

What about poor Mother Earth? Mother Earth is awesome. She can take anything we can dump onto her and transform it back into useable energy. Thus, meditating, energizing, and grounding are far more friendly and useful techniques than dumping and downloading onto another human or a friend. Most people don't have the ability or the knowledge to be able to do what Mother Earth does.

The second type of meditation that we have been talking about is actually more of a guided visualization called the Chakra meditation.

Apart from the standard Pranic meditation already mentioned, this is one of the most useful and important things that you can do for both yourself and your aura. It energizes, grounds, clears, and recharges. The process is typically a simple one of focusing on each of the chakras (psychic energy centers in the body) and cleaning it with white light and then adding the appropriate color to the chakra to strengthen and balance it. The real major benefit of this form of meditation is that it helps to strengthen an aura. Something like an aura exercise. As you know by now, the stronger the aura, the less likely it is to be penetrated and the less likely you are to lose or have your energy taken from you. A chakra visualization is demonstrated in chapter five of this book.

The simplest way to do this type of meditation is to relax, surround yourself in white light, and then focus on each of the colors of the rainbow. This form of color therapy used by some psychologists is a very effective way of doing a form of the Chakra meditation. Do it daily, and even twice a day if you can muster it, as its benefits and effects will be long-lasting.

Chakra is a Sanskrit word for spinning wheel. Eastern societies have known for a long time about the spinning wheels, or chakra energy centers that are within our energy field. Though we have many such energy centers within our energy field, in the new age field we are primarily interested in seven of them. The seven that are said to align the spine.

The first chakra is located at the base of the spine. It's called the root center. This root center is associated with the color red and is responsible for our survival in this physical world. When we clear and energize this center we are improving our own vitality. Emotional issues in our lives that deal with the need to survive typically will indicate a dirty root center.

The second chakra is located just below the belly button and is commonly called the sacral center. This sacral center is associated with the color orange and is responsible for our gut level intuition. It also has a major impact in our creative ability. Those people who claim they aren't creative, they just typically have a dirty sacral center. Additionally, this center affects our abundance or lack of it. Obviously, the more energized and clear this center the more abundance we can expect in our lives.

The third of the seven chakras is referred to as the solar plexus center and is located just above the belly button at the base of the sternum. It is often times associated with the color yellow. This center is responsible for how well our mind operates. It also has an impact on our self-esteem or self worth. People with low self-esteem or who view themselves as being worthless typically have a dirty solar plexus center. Think about it. Solar comes from the sun. The sun deals with the vitality of all life. When there is no sun we find ourselves in darkness. Likewise, when this center is dirty, our own personal sun isn't able to shine and we find ourselves plunged into our own inner world of darkness. Any type of emotional disappointment from a loved one, if we allow it to happen, can result in this center becoming dirty. The easiest way to ensure this doesn't happen is by remembering what was stated earlier about personal boundaries, and how you can't control what happens beyond or outside your own boundaries.

The fourth center is the heart center. It is the center that you hear talked about most often. It's not actually located where the heart is, rather it's located right in the center of the chest. This chakra influences all forms of healing, especially psychic, and also helps our ability to love unconditionally to function. The color most often associated with it is green, but from time to time you may hear people associating the color pink to it. Our psychic ability to feel (called empathy and clairsentience) is also strongly attached to this center.

The fifth center is called the throat center and it is located at the root of the tongue in the back of the throat. It is most often associated with the color blue. This center is one of the most important ones as it is said to deal with our willpower. Likewise, our willpower affects our ability to manifest thoughts, control our thoughts and actions, and self discipline. When this center is dirty we are typically afraid to speak up and tend to want to hide in the background. This center has an important impact on our clairaudient ability or psychic hearing. The more clear and energized this center is, the more likely we are to "hear" information from our inner voice, higher self, and guides.

The sixth center goes by the name brow center. It's more commonly referred to as the third eye center. It is located above the bridge of the nose in-between the two eye brows. This center is usually associated with the color indigo. The more clear and energized this center is, the more developed our clairvoyant ability tends to be. Thus, if you want to see auras, have psychic visions, or see dead people you should spend a majority of your time focusing on this center and filling it with white light, gold light, and indigo light.

The last of the seven is called the crown center. This particular center is located at the top of our head just above the scalp. It's usually associated with the color violet, though sometimes you'll hear people refer to it as being white in color. Both can be used and neither is more right or wrong than the other. This center affects our spirituality. The more clear and energized this center is the more open we are to spiritual insights that go far above and beyond our normal insights and understanding. Additionally, a clear center here helps to keep us in touch with our inner self.

When we talk about colors, it's important to note that what we represent here is not set in stone. The colors you are being given are the normal physical world colors that these particular centers resonate most with. That's not to say that the colors do not change or can't be different. The important thing is that you stick with whatever you initially started with.

Also, since this book is a guide to energy it's important to briefly mention the idea of sound.

Sound is nothing more than energy set to the harmonics of the universe. All sounds resonate with one of the chakra points. Thus, music is very important to us human beings living here in the physical world.

Each chakra point is connected to a pitch or note. When you hear that pitch or note repeatedly, the chakra starts to resonate with it and, by virtue of the laws of resonance, will begin to adjust and open. Thus, even if you aren't good at visualizing the colors of the chakras, by finding a piece of music that is soft and enjoyable and that connects to all notes on the scale, you'll also be working to open your chakra centers and the psychic abilities that are connected to them. This is perhaps one reason why many musicians tend to have more "psychic" and "spiritual" experiences than the "average" person.

Also, while speaking about music and energy, it would do us good to pay attention to how the mood of music affects our being. If you listen to depressing music over and over again you will, no doubt, begin to feel depressed. Likewise, the opposite also holds true here. By listening to a happy and joyful piece of music repeatedly, especially when down or depressed, you will no doubt begin to feel better about yourself and your life and, as such, will notice your life undergoing vast improvement.

3. A good healer

Locating and using an experienced and recommended healer is yet another way to both repair your aura and recharge yourself. A healer can usually locate where the root problems occur, and then go about using energy from the universe to fix holes and tears in the aura and fill you with light energy. A good healer works on many different levels and their effects are more often seen in the emotional, mental, intuitive, and spiritual aspects of your life as opposed to the purely physical, although it has not been uncommon for physical healing to take place when the other aspects of a person finally come into alignment.

Everyone in our psychic development classes is encouraged to find and work with a healer. This is needed to make sure you are in balance. It's hard to learn to control and work with your psychic abilities when you haven't found that inner balance within.

What is the best way to find a good healer?

Here's my advice. Those who are highly recommended are the best to start with. Understand that a healer who thinks that he or she is the only one capable of working with healing energies, or if they seem too egoistic in their work, they won't make for great healing work. Great healing work comes when the healer removes the ego and just simply allows the love and energy to flow from Mother Earth or the Universe through them. Healers should charge for their work just like anyone else, but they should not make blatant claims (nor should psychics for that matter) like "You are cursed and for a small fee I can remove the curse" or "All your chakras are blocked, I can fix that for you for an additional fee." The price should be very clear upfront and there should not be any attempt on the part of the healer (or the psychic) to force you to pay more than the mutually agreed amount.

The healer that you choose to work with should look forward to and be eager to discuss any questions about their work that you may want to ask.

I would like to take a few moments to discuss my own personal experiences with some very different healers who I trust and adore.

The first of these is a young woman that specializes in Tai massage. She also does various forms of angelic healing and has spent a good deal of time studying traditional Chinese Medicine and how to apply it.

My massage sessions with her have been nothing but spectacular. I've never come out of a session with her and not felt ten times better than before I entered it. Her presence in and of itself has a calming and healing effect.

It would seem that many people underestimate the importance of a good massage. It not only helps to release aches and pains, but it also does a great deal to increase the chi, or life force, circulation within your body.

Many times a person will fall asleep while working with a massage therapist. I can attest to several times when I've drifted out of consciousness while beneath the enchanting power of a masseuses hands.

Note that this is a common thing to happen with any healer. Many times we must lose consciousness (via sleep) so that the healing work which is being done can affect not only our physical bodies, but the root of the problems which lie within our emotional, mental, and spiritual bodies. Also, be aware that sometimes our conscious mind only gets in the way and interferes with the healing work which is being done; another reason why drifting into that sleep state isn't necessarily a bad thing.

By now you should realize that a person has four aspects to themselves; a physical one, an emotional one, a mental one, and a spiritual one. A healer works usually with the spiritual, mental, or emotional aspects which then, many times, will result in the physical body improving.

Another healer that I've had the pleasure to work with was a modern day Shaman.

Working with a Shaman can be very different than working with a standard massage therapist. A shaman tends to use a variety of tools to help both you and them enter into deeper states of trance so that they can work to restore balance and harmony to you on all levels of existence. They do this through sacred sound (remember how each note is connected to a chakra point?), sacred smoke (more on smudging later), chanting, working with the energy of the aura itself, and many other methods.

I've seen many a person leave a session with this Shaman with a large smile upon their face and a sense of relief and satisfaction around them. When I would ask them how the session was they would always respond that they've never felt better.

My own sessions with this Shaman were also nothing short of amazing. He would always get right to the root of almost any emotional problem I was having. He then preformed some work to release those emotions and even out the energy flow within my physical and spiritual bodies.

I am fortunate enough to have been able to actually do some private Shamanic lessons with this Shaman. During these lessons he stressed the importance of going within to find answers. He also demonstrated and showed me that breathing was the most important thing that any person can do. It is through taking time to breathe that one allows themselves to enter into the meditative state (commonly called the alpha state).

He was not the first person that I learned the value and benefits of rhythmic breathing from. During my time with the Rosicrucian AMORC I learned a great deal of the value and importance of breath work and how one can use the breath to amplify the healing work they do with others. That brings to mind another healer I had the opportunity to work with. Though he enjoys his privacy and likes to go unnamed, he worked with a healing technique called Quantum Touch.

We use to hold a healing circle monthly, sometimes even weekly, at my store Starchild in Port Charlotte. This particular healer always formed an important part of that circle.

By now you should be asking, "What is Quantum Touch?" According to **quantumtouch.com** "Quantum-Touch is a powerful, yet easy to learn, method of natural healing (or energy healing). Everyone has the innate ability to help ourselves and others. The Quantum-Touch techniques teach us how to focus and amplify life-force energy (or Chi, Bioenergy, Prana) by combining various breathing and energy awareness exercises. QT energy healers learn to amplify and direct the life-force energy, facilitating the body's own healing process. Our love has more impact than we can imagine; the possibilities are truly extraordinary."

Though I personally do not know how to perform Quantum Touch, I do know that Quantum Touch works with the breath. By using various breathing patterns a QT practitioner is apparently able to raise another person's vibration to match their own. While a person is in that raised vibratory state they are capable of feeling what "normal" and "healthy" is and then their own energy field can copy that state thereby restoring them to "healthy."

I've seen this particular healer work what many might call miracles: curing animals to restoring eye sight. There was even one case where a person with cancer was seeing him. To make a long story short, that individual found out that their cancer went into remission. Though nobody can prove that it was the QT which helped with this, that particular individual strongly felt that it was because of his Quantum Touch sessions.

There are actually lots of stories like this one listed at **quantumtouch.com** that are well worth reading and investigating.

Personally I tend to work with two very different forms of healing that end up complimenting each other very nicely. The first is Reiki. Reiki is a Japanese form of healing that has been around, so it is said, since the time of Christ (if not before). It's also one of the most popular healing modalities in the world

I also tend to work with Angelic Touch Therapy. Angelic Touch Therapy involves invoking angels and allowing them to work with a person's energy field.

Both of these healing techniques are independent of each other, but I've personally have had great success using them together.

Understand that the concept of angels helping and interacting with us isn't a new one nor is it specific to any one religion or spiritual belief system. In fact, according to a Gallup poll, over 80% of Americans believe in Angels. Additionally, a poll in Canada has indicated that 66% of Canadians believe in them. A world poll of about 1800 adults indicated that 55% of them believe they had guardian angels and 40% of them believed they had an encounter with an angel.

Perhaps one healer I am still in awe of is a man that worked with a channeled form of healing called sound healing. This particular type of healing is done with Tibetan Bowls and Crystal Bowls. When you lay down to allow this healer and his guides to work with you, it's like going in for a "tune up." Much like changing the oil in your car. Your entire being goes through a shift and core aspects of yourself undergo change and transformation as he and his guide's music works on your entire being.

In the short time I've known him and seen his work I was utterly amazed at a woman who had been suffering from a high degree of back pain since an automobile accident. She went in for a session with the sound healer and an hour later she came out in tears.

"For the first time in years I am actually without pain" she kept saying over and over. Whatever damage that car wreck had done to her energy system, the sounds of the bowls had changed and transformed it into painlessness and lightheartedness.

All of the healers that I mention here work with the same energy. You can call it God, the Universal Consciousness, your Holy Guardian Angel, or even the Architect of the Universe. No matter what you call it, they are working in conjunction with it to allow the holes and damage that has been done to an aura and even the chakra centers themselves to be repaired. They go even beyond that and work on those invisible levels that the majority of humans don't think about. Regardless, they help to restore a person back to balance. I highly recommend all of them and hope you will give one or two of them a try at some point in the future or, at the very least, find someone in your own area that works with a similar modality of healing.

CORE PROTECTION IDEA

In addition to being able to regain your energy, start getting yourself right away into the mind frame that you ALWAYS have control over what you do or don't allow through your auric field. Even when we are blasted or dumped on, we still have that power. It doesn't matter if someone bullies us into letting them in or we feel compelled to share our energy with someone because of various circumstances. No matter what, we still control what we do and don't allow in.

There are some things we want to allow in. For example, we want to allow love into our aura. The emotion and energy of love is very powerful and the more we can accept and share with others the more powerful our own and others' energy fields become.

There are other things we certainly don't want to allow in like some-one else's bad mood. If we allow another person's bad mood to get into our auric field, we begin to feel like crap and we end up entering into a bad mood ourselves. We don't have to allow that to happen. All we need to do is mentally visualize ourselves as having a shield up around us with a door in its center. When we want to allow things in we mentally visualize that door opening. Likewise, when we want to shut out bad moods, anger, and such negative emotions that other people may bombard us with, we only have to mentally visualize that door closing and locking from within, and we will have won half the energy battle.

There are of course many other ways of protecting ourselves and we will look at those in the remaining chapters of this book.

Section II:
Methods and Techniques of Protecting

There are six main methods or techniques of psychically protecting yourself. Within many of these are various sub-methods.

CHAPTER 4

Technique One: Proper Thought

There is nothing more powerful than our own brain. To have prop-er thought is to have won 95% of all battles before they even begin. There are two great books available for people who wish to learn proper thought. The first of these was written in 1910 and is titled *The Science of Getting Rich*. The second book, *Think and Grow Rich*, came in about 1937. Get your hands on one of these books and keep reading and referring to it!

The Science of Getting Rich provides a very simple way of creat-ing wealth and happiness in your life. Despite the fact the overall tone and theme of this book is on acquiring money, the procedure it shows for doing so is the same procedure one can use to help acquire most anything in their life.

Think and Grow Rich is one of the most popular motivational books to have ever been written and is on the bookshelf of many of the most successful people in the world. The book speaks on the power of thought and how to use various methods to apply it to various life situations.

The video *The Secret* is the other place where you can learn a lot about what proper thought is. *The Secret* is a more modern version of these two books. It interviews many successful and wealthy leaders of today's world. All of them show and explain that the primary method they used to get to where they are is proper thought.

The technique of proper thought centers on the Law of Attraction. The universe we live in has certain laws that must be obeyed. For example, the law of gravity states that what goes up must come down. Likewise, the law of attraction is one of the laws of our universe and effectively this law suggests that you can attract or bring towards you whatever it is you happen to dwell upon and think of. Let's look at an example. If you spend the majority of your time dwelling upon the sun and happy thoughts, making money and bringing new enjoyable friends into your life, these things tend to happen. They are far more likely to happen to you because you are allowing yourself to be more open and inviting to them. By the same token, if you spend the majority of your time dwelling upon all the bills you have to pay, the fights that might occur in your life, and the bad news you may end up receiving, you are allowing yourself to be more open and inviting to these things appearing in your life. The Law of Attraction works regardless of if you try to apply the law or not. The only power you have within the context of this law is the power to choose exactly what you spend your time thinking about and dwelling on.

As such, it does well for people to work on centering their life on positive thoughts and spending the vast majority of their time around people who also try to focus their energy and thoughts in a positive direction. Remember this: true friends will always want you to succeed and will not cut you down when you do. If you are a person who is constantly around a lot of negative criticism and your thought patterns are suffering because of it, please do yourself a favor and find a way to either remove that person from your life or to minimize contact with them. It will go a long ways in helping you to keep your faith in yourself strong and as such keep your aura strong.

When you are connected intimately to someone, be it to a friend, spouse or even a family member, it is likely that the two of you, when together, have auras that are connecting to each other. If you live together, this will almost always be even truer. It is virtually impossible for two people to exist in the same environment and not have a common energy field in which they are connected with each other. When you are sharing an energy field so strongly, it is entirely possible for the thoughts of one person to have a dramatic effect on the life of another. Remember, like will always attract like. We don't have to accept that, it just happens! This means that if you have a partner who is constantly thinking bad and nasty things about their child-hood or who visualizes a future full of dread and woe, they will, by the universally mandated law, attract this to themselves. It may not be that it happens directly to them. You see, by being connected in that common energy field, it is entirely possible that what one person is putting out may end up in the other person's life, because they are both sharing that life. When it comes to a point that this appears to be happening over and over again, it is the duty and responsibility of the person who is making every attempt possible to bring positivity into their life to make adjustments within that relationship. To set ground rules and boundaries on what is and isn't acceptable. If, for whatever reason, there can be no cooperation to set these ground rules, then that person will need to be cut loose.

As painful as it is for the human emotions to accept, there are certain people who, for a number of reasons, constantly want to be held back or who do not wish to advance to their next level or even phase of life. No matter how hard a positive thinking person tries, if they attempt to bring that person up with them, because of the natural laws of gravity, the person who is at a lower level will almost always drag the person down from the higher level. Only if a person who is at that lower level is truly seeking to improve and evolve or advance, will the higher level person have any remote chance at helping to bring them up to the same level with them. If that desire is not there, it is far better to let the lower level person go, to cut them totally and completely out of your life, so that the higher level person may continue with their growth pattern.

What about compassion? What about unconditional love? To let such a person go is truly the most remarkable act of universal love and compassion for the self. By letting such a person go, they will be forced to learn a hard lesson about the importance of how they use their energy and how it is having an effect on those around them. This point is engraved even more so, when the lower level person sees or realizes what they could have had if only they would have allowed themselves to evolve with rather than against their friend/sister/brother/spouse etc. Remember this: having unconditional love and compassion means saying: "I love you so much, that I desire from the depths of my soul to see you improve, and I know that by continuing to be involved with your life you will never make an attempt to be the person you were possible of being if I am not removed from your life."

A person should spend some time each day on visualizing and focusing on their aura being totally healthy and strong. Think about what your life will be like once you obtain whatever success you are seeking and looking for. Let nothing or no one detour you from these thoughts.

Tell yourself that from now on, you are taking total and complete responsibility for your life, both the good and the bad. If there is something you don't like, figure out how you've attracted it to yourself and then do the work (both mental and the physical actions needed) to change the situation. Until you are capable of doing this, accepting that you bring both the bad and good into your life, you will never be able to fully train yourself to have proper thought. The same is true for those who are strongly connected to you. They must do this work with you, or else there will come a point and time where, both for you and them to continue to grow, you will need to go separate ways.

Let no separation ever leave you with bad or negative feelings or thoughts. Every relationship and connection you have to another person in this world is one where both individuals are learning something from each other and usually multiple things from each other. As long as you've learned something from that individual, then they have served a purpose to you and you to them. At a higher level, beyond what most humans can even ponder, this action or behavior has even greater implications. As individuals grow, so does the world's, and in turn the whole universal soul grows and evolves. Ultimately this can force the cosmic soul to evolve, which allows for the evolution of the form of God itself. This, my friend, is the reason that proper thought in and of itself becomes so largely important. It serves both to defend on a purely psychic and energy level here in the physical world, while at the same time helps to promote and raise the consciousness of the God form itself.

My guides and I realize that these concepts of God and the consciousness of God are a bit tricky right now. We know that some of you who have been within this field for a long time will already understand what is being said and that those of you who are new and just sitting foot into this field may be highly confused. Please trust us when we say that this concept will be explored in much more depth in future writings. Until then, if you must conquer your thirst for knowledge, consider reading the beginning chapters of the book *Modern Magickk* by Donald Michael Kraig or read the entire book *Chicken Qabalah* by Lon Milo Duquette.

In *Modern Magickk*, Donald Kraig shows how every person in the world is connected to the greater intelligence that most of us call God. In *Chicken Qabalah* Lon Duquette explores, with comedy, what is referred to as the tree of life, a system of Jewish Mysticism. He breaks it down into lay person terms and makes it easy to understand how the parts (all humans) are all connected to a greater whole (God).

Affirmations are a terrific way to build that positive image up in your mind, on both the conscious and subconscious level. In fact, you should have at least one affirmation you can start saying immediately when you discover that you are having negative thoughts. It takes only a thought to produce a change within our mind, and a positive thought will always be 100 times more powerful than a negative one. So learn to catch your bad thoughts and then immediately redirect your thoughts toward something good. This can be the image of someplace or someone, or (as has been mentioned earlier) an affirmation.

Sample Affirmations

- *I am fully and totally loved by the great universe and only positive thoughts, words, and actions come to me.*
- *Love surrounds me and I embrace it.*
- *I feel at peace with myself and thank the universe for it.*
- *My aura is strong and healthy, and radiates with the power of universal protection.*
- *I am a God/Goddess and am capable of having anything I desire.*

- *People love and adore me and all desire to be embraced by my presence.*
- *I am healthy and strong and feel at my best each and every day.*
- *I attract money and success to me by the second.*
- *I deserve wealth and prosperity and find that I easily attract it into my life.*

The key to affirmations has nothing to do with how many times you say it and everything to do with what you think and how much energy you put into what you are saying. I can keep saying "Love surrounds me and I embrace it", but if my mind is not focusing on the words and the images being created by what is being said, then I am really gaining nothing from repeating the affirmation.

Meditation, as motioned earlier, is the one method of training the mind to focus. When you use affirmation with a focused or meditative mind, this is when you start to experience the real power of what the affirmations have to offer.

The exception to this is when you have an affirmation that is being repeated prior to sleep. This allows the affirmation, provided you are focusing on it as you drift into sleep, to work on a very profound subconscious level. Some would call this autosuggestion.

Autosuggestion is the process of repeating something with intent in your conscious mind with the desire to incorporate it within the subconscious mind. It is really true, we do listen to ourselves. As such, it is imperative that you speak only words of love and kindness to the self or, if one must be critical: to approach the criticism from a growth-oriented and evolution- oriented perspective as opposed to a hate-oriented perspective.

Building your faith, determination, and self confidence with this technique is so very important to your psychic self defense. It was Napoleon Hill in his book *Think and Grow Rich* on page 41 of the revised edition who said, "There is nothing, right or wrong, which belief plus burning desire cannot make real. These qualities are free to everyone." Always make an attempt to focus on the positive while not give energy to the negative and you will be well on your way to winning the energy battles that most people become consumed in. Also know when it's time to move on and not allow others to act as hindrances to you.

Another thing that many people like to do is add affirmations into their meditations and guided visualizations. One of my absolute favorite guided visualizations that I call Kyoto Gardens is included here for your enjoyment.

It is rather long and so it's not recommended that, at first, you try memorizing the whole thing. The first few times you do it, it may be easier for you if you have a friend read it to you while you do the visualizations or, even better, if you record your own voice saying it and then do the guided meditation to your own voice.

Within this guided meditation/visualization there are several affirmations. Some of them are straightforward and easy to pick out, but there are also many symbolic affirmations that occur as well.

Kyoto Gardens

Take three deep breaths to become calm and centered.

We are going to count from 1 to 10. With each number you will feel yourself going deeper within. As we count each number you will also feel yourself becoming more and more relaxed. Let's begin.

1. Relax the top of your head. Relax your forehead. Wrinkle it. Release. Wrinkle again. Release. Roll your head on your shoulders, first in one direction.... then in the other. Swallow to release any tension in your throat. Take a few moments to feel the accumulation of relaxation in your head, face, neck, and shoulders.

2. Imagine a cloud of white light entering into the top of your head. Then watch as it slowly begins to wrap itself around your brain, cradling it like a baby. Feel your brain wave patterns begin to slow as your whole being relaxes.

3. Take a deep breath. As you exhale, feel a wave of relaxation go from the top of your head, all the way through your body and out from the soles of your feet.

4. Focus on your feet, ankles, and toes. Feel all the muscles relax. Tighten them. Release. Tighten again. Release. Feel relaxation gathering in your feet.

5. Focus on your legs. The upper and lower. Focus on the calf and thigh muscles and mentally tell them to relax and sleep. Feel them obey you.

6. Focus on your lower torso and all the muscles and organs inside. Tell all of them to relax and let go. Feel the tension slip away as they obey and begin to drift into a deep relaxation.

7. Focus on your upper torso and all the muscles and organs inside. Tell all of them to relax and let go. Feel the tension melt away as they begin to drift into a deep and gentle state of relaxation.

8. Focus on your back. The whole back. From the upper to the lower. Imagine a pair of white hands appearing behind you and watch as they slowly, but firmly, begin to massage your back. Feel all tension in your back slip away as you relax in their soft and loving energy. Mentally, thank the hands and then whisper to your whole back and ask it to relax and sleep.

9. Bring your attention to your arms, hands, wrists, and fingers. Tighten these. Release. Feel the difference. Tighten again and release. Mentally tell all the muscles here to relax and let go. Feel them obey.

10. Allow yourself to be in an alpha state. This is a state where your body is relaxed, but your mind is alert and awake. Follow your breath for a few moments as you contemplate being in this state of deep, yet peaceful, relaxation.

Imagine yourself standing at the gate of a beautiful, serene garden. Behind you, the bustle and noise of Kyoto has already started to fade, blending with the subtle sweep and rush of the gentle river beyond the gate. You close your eyes and listen, letting the soft, rhythmic lap of water gradually wash away the worries and the outer noise, drawing you forward through the gate. The warmth of the sun is a gentle kiss of greeting and an invitation to step into the serenity and abundance that awaits your awakening presence. You feel yourself being drawn into the vital life force that flows around you and realize that you are a part of this energy and beauty and have always been.

Now accept the invitation and step through the gate into the peace of the garden. You open your senses to all that is around you, feeling the supportive energy of earth and stone, hearing the healing ripple of still waters and taking in the energizing light and warmth of the sun as it bathes your spirit in radiant energy. Before you, a silvered wooden pathway extends to the heart of the garden. You leave your shoes at the gate and walk along, the weathered wood smooth and warm beneath your bare feet. With each step, you can feel the garden opening to you, accepting you as part of its essence.

As you walk along the path, you imagine the spirits of those who created these gardens walking with you, welcoming you to share the beauty and serenity of their work. All around you, you see others like yourself opening their senses to the wonder and vitality that is a part of them. As you pass, they look up to meet your gaze, greeting you with a warm smile that welcomes you and brings you closer to the realization that you deserve this peace and tranquility because you are YOU. There is no pressure to earn acceptance here - you are accepted and loved and respected for being the person that you are.

You walk through the garden, taking in all that is around you. To the left and to the right, beds of gray gravel form whorls and patterns, shapes that flow and reform as you pass them. Peace and tranquility flows along the gentle lines and curves, lapping outwards to engulf you with welcoming warmth. You close your eyes for a moment and simply bask in the sensation of pure acceptance and listen to the gentle ebb and flow of lapping water that lies ahead of you. In your mind's eye, the patterns of the rocks and the rhythm of the water blend and you realize that they are one and the same. The rhythms, the patterns, the warmth, the vitality - they are all a part of you that you can touch and shape whenever you want. You take a slow deep breath, filling your senses with the scent of clean earth and crisp citrus, then open your eyes and move forward along the path.

Just ahead, the wooden path descends in a gentle slope to an open sward of close-cropped emerald grass surrounding a round pool of glistening water. The gentle lapping of the water underscores a faint, playful chiming that comes from the side. At the very edge of the water, a profusion of vibrant flowers grow on low bushes and hedges. Brilliant pink lotuses and warm peach peonies invite you closer to examine them and study their structure. You step closer and the sweet, earthy scent of life washes over you, filling you with a sense of well-being and tranquility. You note the patterns and the shape of the blooming flowers, the way the colors and velvety textures fit together, wrapping and enfolding and protecting that which lies within. As you study its form and structure, the closed petals gently open, unfolding one by one to offer you the brilliant heart of the flower and you realize that this is your life - offering you all that is most beautiful and wonderful. You only need to reach out your hand and take what you want. Like the flowers, all the good things that you want are plentiful and replenish themselves when you open yourself to understand what it is that you want from life.

Step back from the bushes now, and take in the garden in its entirety. Rock and earth, leaf and bud, water and wood all fit together as a seamless whole. Close your eyes again and listen for the sounds of life around you and realize that this is all yours for you to take whenever you are ready. You are not a visitor to this garden, it is inside you and a part of you, and you are all that you see and feel around you. You are the warmth of the sun and the gentle caress of the lapping water. The amazing beauty of each flower is part of you. The graceful arch of the willow and the playful twinkling melody of the wind chimes are part of you. You are grace and beauty, warmth and welcome, strength and tenderness all in one.

Let the garden fill you, know and believe that you can feel this way every moment of your life. From now on, you will focus on the good and the positive energies that flow inside you, and those energies will reflect to all those around you. As you make your way back up the wooden pathway, you know that you are not leaving the garden behind you, but taking it with you, for it is as much part of you as you are part of this life.

Now, we will count backwards from 10 to 1. When we reach 1, you will return to the waking beta state of mind, taking all your experiences with you.

10.
9.
8.   Wiggle your fingers
7.
6.   Wiggle your toes
5.
4.   Stretch
3.   Take a deep breath in
2.   Let it out
1.   Allow yourself to return to the room.

GOAL SETTING

In addition to working with positive affirmations and keeping your thoughts focused in a positive direction, it's also important that you use your visualization techniques in conjunction with goal setting.

The majority of people in our world *think* they set goals for themselves. The problem is, these goals tend to have the New Year's Resolution Syndrome. That is, wonderful great thoughts about what one would like to do, but it's only a thought and nothing ever becomes of it.

When you truly set a goal and work towards achieving it, you allow yourself to be driven by an inner passion. This inner passion results in the right circumstances being drawn to a person and, more importantly, the right actions being taken in order to capitalize on those circumstances.

A goal need not be easily accomplished. A goal must, however, be within the realms of what your subconscious mind believes to be possible. If you consciously don't think it's possible to achieve, then there is no way that your subconscious mind will allow you to do so. Even if you consciously believe you can achieve a goal, if there is some aspect of your subconscious working against you, it can make reaching the end result very difficult, if not impossible.

A goal should be written and kept in a place where you can look back over and review it often. It needs not to be shared with others, unless those that you are sharing it with are going to be totally and completely supportive in your efforts of achieving the goal.

The following exercise is designed to help you set a future goal in such a manner that you'll be using positive affirmations and visualizations combined with strong passion and emotion to be able to achieve the goal in the future.

Step One: Write down something you want to achieve that you consciously believe is within the realm of possibility.

Ex. Someone works in a business where they see clients regularly. That person wants to be booked out at least a week in advance. They don't think that's impossible by any means. So they write here. *"I want to be booked out a week in advance."*

Step Two: Write down what you'll feel emotionally as a result of this goal being accomplished.

Ex. *I will be filled with joy, success, and contentment.*

Step Three: Write down what life will be like once this goal is accomplished.

Ex. *I will be coming to the office happier. I will be helping more people and feeling better about the work that I perform. I will be able to go home feeling proud of myself.*

Step Four: Now, taking these three things into consideration write down an affirmation in the present tense.

Ex. *I am filled with joy, success, and contentment because I am booked out up to a week in advance. I leave the office feeling happier and having a sense of pride in knowing that I am helping more people build a better life for themselves.*

Step Five: Add a time frame, again as though it's in the present tense. Again, the trick here is to be realistic according to your own conscious mind. If you don't believe it to be possible, it certainly won't be. It doesn't matter how far in advance you make the date.

Ex. *It's six months from (enter today's date). I find myself filled with joy, success, and contentment because I am booked out up to a week in advance. I leave the office feeling happier and having a sense of pride in knowing that I am helping more people build a better life for themselves.*

The goal is now set. Now we must attach the passion to it. To do this we use a technique that Anthony Robins and many other people that work with NLP (stands for neuro linguist programming). A technique which goes by the name anchoring.

To do this we must first think of an experience in our life that has brought to us a feeling of total joy and bliss; a moment which we might identify as being one of the best and greatest moments of our life.

Once we have defined this moment we need to sit with our eyes closed and remember this moment in as much detail as we possibly can; making an attempt to totally relive that moment of complete bliss and joy.

By doing this several times, over and over again, we plant a seed. A seed which, provided we do not let negativity and doubt intervene, will beyond any shadow of a doubt take form and being to take shape in our lives.

. . . . . .ACTION. . . .

It's important to note that no matter how much we use positive affirmations, no matter how much we work to set future goals, and no matter how much we work to think only in a positive manner. . . . . Life doesn't happen simply through thought alone. There must be concrete physical actions that accompany the thought process. Without action, that which we think can never really fully and truly manifest here in the physical world.

This takes us to our next topic of importance.

CHAPTER **5**

Technique Two: Physical Actions & the Physical Body

Just as having proper thought is important, so too is understanding that there are very real physical actions that you can do in order to help protect yourself from negative energy.

Start by folding your hands so that the fingers are interlaced. This very simple action closes off a majority of the energy circuits within the human body. When the circuits are closed, no matter how weak the aura is, you aren't going to get much energy from a person. In fact, if you do this around someone who is complaining (they are downloading or seeking to take your energy), you will discover that you will be able to actively listen to the person without feeling as taxed as you would otherwise.

Generally speaking, what ends up happening is that the person who is downloading or seeking to induce fear ends up becoming unconsciously frustrated by the lack of energy available. When it comes to that point they usually quickly end the conversation and move on in an attempt to get the energy from elsewhere.

The same can happen when you cross your ankles, legs, or arms. Crossing the arms, particularly, can be a great aid in shutting off the heart center and closing down the emotional energy field.

Anyone interested in learning fundamental principals in psychic protection from energy would do well to study the behavior of a rebellious young child.

A young child often finds themselves in an energy battle with their parents. The parent typically wants the child to behave in a certain way or perform a certain task and normally they attempt to get the child to do this by virtue of inducing fear in the child.

While this is not the forum for discussing parenting techniques and energy involvement with them, this is a great time to look at the actions that most children unconsciously fall into when they find themselves caught in an energy battle with a parent.

The young child will usually fold their arms, stomp their feet, and totally avoid eye contact with the parent. Some will even turn their back to the parent. Regardless, they are unconsciously attempting to protect their own energy field through such behaviors.

This doesn't mean that a parent shouldn't discipline their children; rather it is simply another way of looking at energy and how it's constantly playing out in our lives.

It's also important to remember that the left side and back of the body are naturally receptive and the front and right side of the body are naturally generative. When involved in a conversation with someone who seems to be attempting to gain an upper hand (energetically speaking), make an attempt to only look at their left eye with your right eye. This will give you energy leverage. At the very least it makes it more possible for you to be able to hold your own ground.

Be aware that you can also take your right hand and place it over the back of your neck at any time to stop an inflow or outflow of energy. Think of how much better our family man Bill would have been had he done this while in the traffic jam. The back of your neck is the most receptive area on your body.

"Why?" you may ask.

Think of it this way. At the front of your neck is your throat chakra. Remember the chakras? We know that the throat center deals with our will power. The back of the neck is also linked into the throat chakra. As such, it is the back of the neck that most easily allows energy to access your will. When negative energy has access to the root of your will it can quickly cause you problems and easily allow others to link into and suck your energy.

Not only will putting your hand on the back of your neck protect you on an energy level, but many times it will actually allow you to regenerate energy if you focus on white light going through your hand into the back of your neck.

This brings in another interesting example. Ponder for a moment a young lady that is just starting to date. Men end up doing two different things that have a powerful impact upon her energy field and, as such, her personal energy.

The first of these is the way that they look at her. Whenever one person looks another from top to bottom they are lowering that person's energy field. This may well be quite unconscious, but nevertheless, this lowering of the field makes it easier to steal energy, and to manipulate that person.

You can try an experiment with a friend or two.

Have your friend stand a few feet away from you holding their dominant arm straight out to their side. Have them hold that dominant arm up. Tell them that their job is to resist you. Go and attempt to push the arm down. They should do fairly well at resisting your efforts.

Now, take a few steps back. As you walk toward your friend; use your eyes to look them from top to bottom. Don't look from bottom to top, just top to bottom.

This time as you attempt to push their arm down you'll discover that their resistant efforts, to their, and perhaps even your amazements, will fall short. Why? Using merely your eyes, you have sent an unconscious signal to your friend that you are more dominant then they are and have thus affected their auric energy field.

Pretty scary isn't it? Think about all the different ways that people look at you each and every day. You must now ponder how many are acting to lower your energy field and how many are acting to help aid it.

Just as looking from top to bottom can lower an energy field, looking from bottom to top can raise or restore energy. There are many times when I will be co-teaching or lecturing with someone and as I start to notice or feel them running low on energy, I will begin to look at them and scan their body from their toes up to their heads. In almost all occasions the co-instructor will regain energy or feel a rush of energy as they move forward into their next topic.

Let's return to our earlier example of the young lady who is dating. The other thing that many men will do is walk up to her, begin to start some friendly conversation with her, and then slip their arm around the back of her neck. This is not good!

Remember, the neck is the most receptive point on the physical body. When another person puts their arm around your neck or grabs a hold of the back of your neck, they are far more easily able to will you into listening to, or believing them.

Physical exercise is also important. Any type of physical activity or exercise raises the vibration of the physical human body. As our vibration rises we are not usually influenced or affected by lower vibrations. Additionally, it is not at all uncommon to find yourself entering into a meditative (focused mind) state during strenuous physical activity. This can be a good form of meditation that can aid in the restoration of your energy.

Before we go on, we should take a few moments to discuss what we mean by the concept of lower and higher vibration.

When a person is filled with happy and positive emotions and is feeling at their best, their vibration and energy is said to be high. The reverse is also true. When a person is feeling angry, depressed, and unhappy their vibration and energy is said to be low.

When we have a low vibration it tends to be much easier for other negative energies to affect us. Why? The reason it's easier for negative energy to affect us when we have a lower vibration is because we are much more inviting to it. This goes right along with the idea that like attracts like.

When our vibration is high, we tend to be less affected by negative energy. It's almost like we are literally higher than the negative energy, so it passes right by us.

Additionally, physical exercises does a great deal to help clear, clean, strengthen, open, and develop the chakra centers. This is one reason why the total mind-body–spirit connection is emphasized in our field. By working with all aspects of these three areas we are optimizing ourselves.

Separate from this, you should also be aware that as you come into contact with people you form energy links to them, and them to you. The closer you are to someone, the stronger that energy link is. To a clairvoyant such links usually appear as energy tubes going between you and the other person. There are times when having these links, or tubes, is not healthy. Sometimes, by having such a link, a person has merely to think of you and they are capable of tapping into your energy source. When this happens it is a good idea to not only cut these tubes on a psychic level (see technique four: protecting psychically), but to literally visualize the link between you and them and cut through it with your hand.

Likewise, when you are around someone and they seem to be downloading or making you feel uncomfortable, it is okay and, in fact, appropriate, to excuse yourself and literally break the energy connection with that person by moving to a different room or even ending a phone conversation. You will probably want to visualize the tube and cut it, as mentioned above, and in technique four, as well.

Breaking that connection by physically removing yourself from the other's presence is important to grasp though. Many of us, for whatever reason, feel that it's rude to do so and as such we let certain people use us. We and we alone, are responsible for our own energy. It is up to us to know ourselves and how much energy we can give before we become totally drained and are of no good to ourselves. When we are clearly reaching that point, boundary, or limit we must excuse ourselves until a later date and time.

Something else you can do is, as suggested by a friend, spend some time looking at yourself in the mirror. You can actually use the raising/lowering of the eyes to have an impact and effect on your own energy. Thus, when feeling drained of energy, you can excuse yourself to a restroom and spend a few moments looking at yourself and raising your own energy.

EXERCISE

Exercise plays a very important role in not only our health, but also our energy field. It's well known that the healthier we are, the more energy we tend to have. Yet, there are also specific exercises that affect chakras and as such enhance those areas of our life. Before we take a look at those I need to briefly take the time to remind everyone that, as with any exercise program, it's advisable that you consult a physician prior to jumping in and doing these. This is especially true if you are or have suffered from serious health injuries or problems in the past.

Now, from bottom to top, here are the exercises for various chakra points.

- Root Center: Marching in place, stomping, and squats
- Sacral Center: Pelvic thrusts, pelvic circles
- Solar Plexus Center: Dancing, twisting left and right
- Heart Center: Push ups, hugging yourself, back arches
- Throat Center: Signing, stretching the neck, neck rolls
- Third Eye Center: Rubbing the third eye in a circular motion, moving and focusing your eyes in each of the four directions (up/down/left/right)
- Crown Center: Rubbing the crown center in a circular motion

Stretching of all types also helps to open up energy blockages to allow energy to more freely move throughout the body.

DIET

You're going to hear a lot of different things about diet. Some sources are going to tell you that you should try to maintain a vegetarian diet, as vegetables are the most pure with energy and eating just vegetables will raise your vibration. Other sources will tell you that meat is an important element of your diet. It's useful for grounding and helping you keep both feet on the ground. Still other sources will tell you that fasting is important and it must be done so many times per year in order to cleanse and detoxify the body.

What do I think? I think it really doesn't matter what you eat so long as you are in tune with your own body and know what your body needs and you honor that.

A friend of mine, who is a Shaman, once told me that "If you think you're eating crap when you eat, then you're eating crap. If you eat the greasiest thing in the world and think that it's good for you, the body will honor it as being good."

Additionally, when we speak of right diet what we are referring to is what's right for you as an individual. Remember, no two people are the same and as such no two people will ever need the same dietary requirements. Learn what works for you and your body and then work with that.

Water is very important though. It has been said that a person should drink 8 glasses of 8oz of water a day. I say you should be drinking water constantly throughout the day. Every morning it is wise to start the morning with a small warm glass of water. This gets the system running. As you drink water throughout the day you help to return the physical body to its most natural elemental form, that of water. (The human body and in fact much of the world is primarily composed of the energy known as water). This also helps to cleanse the body and keeps the energy running and circulating through it.

Three meals a day are also essential. Though we as human beings are many times tempted to skip one of these three meals, having three balanced meals a day is important for our health and well being. Exactly what you eat at those three meals lies within the dominion of listening to, honoring, and knowing your body.

The Food Journal

How do you learn to listen to your body and honor what it wants and needs? The easiest way to start this process is to keep a journal handy. Every time you eat, record in the journal what you are eating and the time of day you are eating it. Leave enough space after to record how the mood, mind, and body reacted to that food.

Thus, if you find yourself feeling depressed an hour after a particular meal, go back and write this down in the space you left. If you find yourself having stomach issues, write that down. If you feel happy, elated, and great - make a note of this. Through cross referencing and looking back over your journal you'll start to see patterns. Those patterns are the system and way that your body speaks to you. You can then begin to honor your body by eating those things that it wants/enjoys the most and cutting out those things which seem to have a negative impact. In time, you'll find your energy improving along with your state of mind.

Obviously, the idea so far has been to maintain a balanced lifestyle. Have the proper state of mind and get adequate physical exercise. While doing these two things keep in mind the importance of having an affirmation available to immediately change your thought patterns and uplift your mood. Also, always keep in mind that you can freely and effortlessly close your energy circuits to help keep your energy from being accessible from outside sources, regardless of the state the aura is in.

CHAPTER 6

Technique Three: Strengthening the Aura

Remember, the best method of psychic protection is to ensure that you have a healthy and strong aura to begin with. When your aura is healthy and strong, it won't have any holes through which energy can leak out, and you'll be feeling more positive and upbeat as a result.

There are four primary exercises that I use to help strengthen my own aura.

EXERCISE ONE: BASIC AURA BUILDING

Step One: Begin by taking three deep breaths to relax and center.

Step Two: Focus on the earth energy beneath you. Visualize, with intention, this energy coming up out of the earth and making a large bubble around you.

Step Three: Watch as this bubble turns blue.

Step Four: Visualize white light energy raining down outside the bubble, so that everywhere outside the bubble looks brilliantly white. At the same time, see a white spec in your chest expanding outward within the bubble filling the bubble with white light energy.

At this point you should have a blue earth energy bubble around you, white bright light glowing outside the bubble, and bright white light radiating within the bubble.

Step Five: See silver sparkles raining down both outside and inside the bubble. One of the best ways to do this is to visualize a fairy with silver dust sprinkling it both inside and around the bubble.

Step Six: Visualize a holy symbol of protection being traced on your forehead and feel it radiate strength.

These six steps if done daily will gradually help to strengthen the aura field. Additionally, these six steps can be performed at any time when you feel you might need extra protection from others' energy. It does a great job at keeping your energy in and stopping other people's energy from influencing or affecting you.

EXERCISE TWO: CHAKRA

There are many types of visualizations that can lead to opening and clearing the chakra. What follows is one that I especially enjoy doing, and which you may adapt into your own lifestyle.

Step One: Prepare a warm bath or shower.

Step Two: Soak in the bath or relax under the shower.

Step Three: Imagine the water as a bright white light surrounding you.

Step Four: See this white water entering and filling your root center. Watch as the center turns red and spins, throwing off all the dirt that it has collected.

Step Five: See this red flow up and into your sacral center. Watch as the center turns orange and spins, throwing off all the dirt that it has collected.

Step Six: See this orange flow up and into your solar plexus center. Watch as the center turns yellow and spins, throwing off all the dirt that it has collected.

Step Seven: See this yellow flow up and into your heart center. Watch as the center turns green and spins, throwing off all the dirt that it has collected.

Step Eight: See this green flow up and into your throat center. Watch as the center turns blue and spins, throwing off all the dirt that it has collected.

Step Nine: See this blue flow up and into your third eye center. Watch as the center turns indigo and spins, throwing off all the dirt that it has collected.

Step Ten: See this indigo flow up and into the crown center. Watch as the center turns purple and spins, throwing off all the dirt that it has collected.

Step Eleven: Feel the water wash over your body and carry away any negative energy that is still hanging around the centers.

Step Twelve: Come back to your physical senses by opening your eyes.

Remember, the importance of doing the chakra meditation is that this form of color therapy balances, opens, and clears the energy centers within your body. It is when your chakras are clear, balanced, and opened, that your vibration rises, which as mentioned above, allows you to be less affected or influenced by negative forces around you.

EXERCISE THREE: THE LESSER BANISHING RITUAL OF THE PENTAGRAM (LBRP)

The LBRP is a powerful exercise that not only charges and strengthens your aura, but creates a circle of protection around and within you at the same time. It is the next logical step after having mastered standard meditation and chakra meditation.

The LBRP should be done nightly before bed and at anytime when you are feeling overcome by the day's stress and prior to entering stressful situations.

Part One: Cabbalistic Cross
Step One: Begin by facing east. Take three deep neutral breaths to relax and center yourself.

Step Two: Close your eyes. Focus on a ball of gold light above your head. Inhale deeply, and as you exhale bring this ball of light down into your head. Reaching up, make a cross (top to bottom, right to left) and chant the God name "Yod Hey Vow Hey."

The words *Yod Hey Vow Hey* is Hebrew. Though this may not be the correct Hebrew spelling, it is written in the form in which I was taught to say it. The hope is that this allows others to have an easier time with pronunciation of the words.

Step Three: Visualize the symbol for Libra (the scales to represent balance) in the center of your chest. Take a deep breath in and as you exhale. Feel the gold light move from the head down into the chest. Watch those scales glow brightly. Make a cross and chant the God name "Yod Hey Vow Hey."

Step Four: Visualize the astrological symbol for the planet Mars (the universal symbol for the male gender, a circle with a pointed arrow) on your right side. Visualize a gold light forming around this symbol and growing brighter. Inhale deeply, and as you exhale see this light brilliantly shining. Reach over and make a cross and chant "Yod Hey Vow Hey."

Step Five: Visualize the astrological symbol for Jupiter (looks almost like the number four) on your left shoulder. Take a deep breath and as you exhale feel the gold light on your right move from right to left. Watch Jupiter glow brightly. Make a cross and chant the God name "Yod Hey Vow Hey."

Step Six: Cross your arms over your chest so that the right hand rests on the left shoulder, and the left hand on the right shoulder. Bow slightly. Take a deep breath in, and as you exhale feel an explosion of gold light coming from the center of your chest and outward. Chant the name of God "Yod Hey Vow Hey."

Part Two: Banishing of energy
Step Seven: Rise. Make a banishing pentagram in the air towards the east. To do this, visualize the point of the pentagram starting at your left hip, going diagonally right towards the top of your head. Now you are going diagonally right from the top of the head to your right hip. Then draw the line going from the right hip diagonally upwards towards the left shoulder. Draw the next part by moving from the left shoulder straight across

to the right shoulder. Finish it by drawing a diagonal line from the right shoulder down towards the left hip. We break it up here, but with practice you should eventually be able to do it all in one motion. After finishing this chant the name "Yod Hey Vow Hey,"

Step Eight: Turn towards the south. Draw a banishing pentagram in the air. Chant "E-Hi-Uh."
This, as with all the Hebrew words in this exercise, is used primarily as additional names for that god force energy. Also, as with yod hey vow hey, the way it is written is the way I was taught to say it, not necessarily the correct Hebrew spelling for the word.

Step Nine: Turn towards the west. Draw a banishing pentagram in the air. Chant "Ad-oh-Nie".

Step Ten: Turn towards the north. Draw a banishing pentagram in the air. Chant "Ah-Glah."

Step Eleven: Turn back towards the east. Again draw a banishing pentagram, but this time, in silence.

Part Three: Calling forth the angelic protectors.
Step Twelve: Facing east, visualize a bright yellow light filling the room. Feel a rush of air blowing in your face. Call forth "To the east, Raphael." Visualize an angel with a staff glowing green.

Step Thirteen: Facing south, visualize a bright red light filling the room. Feel the heat of fire around you. Call forth "To the south, Me-Ki-El" Visualize an angel with a sword, saluting you.

Step Fourteen: Facing west, visualize a bright blue light filling the room and feel the mist of water around you. Call forth "To the west, Gabriel." Visualize an angel appearing and blowing a horn.

Step Fifteen: Facing north, visualize a bright gold light filling the room See a mountain of earth form in the east. Call forth "To the north, Urieal." See an angel appear on top of the mountain carrying some scales.

Step Sixteen: Facing east again, raise your hands in the air and proclaim. "About me flames the pentagram, within me shines the six-rayed star."

Part Four: Repeat of the Cabbalistic Cross
Finally, to end this exercise, repeat part one.

Let's take a moment to discuss the six-rayed star and pentagram The six-rayed star, also called the Star of David, represents the union of opposites. It's a representation of the heaven and the earth joining together. It's also a representation of the male and female energy coming together as one.

When a person puts themselves in the center of this symbol they are, in essence, making a very strong connection to their higher self.

A lot of people will also find it somewhat confusing that I'm using a combination of Judeo-Christian imagery and pagan symbols. The confusion will begin to fade away when one does some research on early Christian symbolism, which included the pentagram. Among the things the pentagram has represented include the first five books of the bible and the five wounds of Christ. In fact, it was the Roman emperor Constantine that was most noted for wearing the pentagram, then a symbol of Christ's wounds, attached to and with jewelry.

According to templestudy.com, it wasn't until around 1856 that a Roman Catholic priest by the name of Eliphas Levi made all good representations with the pentagram bad. He would end up adapting the inverted pentagram as a symbol of evil whereas previously no such connection or connotation was ever made.

Because of this act, the symbol would eventually become associated with paganism and, worse, satanic acts.

I use the symbolism of the pentagram, because for the longest time it has had an association with not only good, but the ultimate form of good. This makes the connection with the imagery of the angels' sounder.

Angels, though, are not purely Christian either. In fact, most major religions have some form and acknowledgement of the angelic race.

The pentagram, Star of David, and angels along with the Hebrew words all work beautifully together to make a ceremony that brings a high level of protection.

EXERCISE FOUR: MIDDLE PILLAR

This is considered an advanced exercise and should only be attempted when the other three have been mastered and have become part of your daily routine.

The Middle Pillar exercise is commonly taught to intermediate students in mystery schools and magick schools. It works with the spiritual energy gates (not the same as the chakras) located within your aura. Please exercise caution if you are going to be attempting this for the first time and, again, please do not attempt until the other two exercises have been fully mastered.

The energy gates are locations within the aura that are closely linked to the chakras. The chakras are an eastern philosophy whilst the energy or spirit gates are a spiritualism concept.

The spirit/energy gates are locations within the human aura where a great deal of spiritual energy flows to and from. Opened, cleaned, and cleared chakras will help in the amount of energy that is capable of flowing through these said gates/energy centers. The energy which flows through them has a different function then that which operates within the chakras.

The energy which operates through the chakra affects us on all levels. The energy which flow through the spirit/energy gates affects us primarily on a "psychic" and spiritual level. It allows us to raise our energy to better be able to connect with angels, guides, and those that have crossed over. It also allows us to transmute that spiritual energy into physical energy. When our own spiritual energy is at a high we are less subjective to the negative vibrations of the world around us, for those vibrations are then operating on a different level than our stronger higher vibrations.

The reason this exercise should be saved until later in development and is not recommended for the beginner is because the amount of energy that can flow and circulate through a persons essence may be a bit more then what they are able to handle. They may not be prepared for the strength/power of the energy. Neither might they be ready for the resulting consequences of achieving such a high vibration too soon in their development and learning. Hearing voices and seeing spiritual energies when one is ready is one thing, but to have it thrust upon one when they are just starting to understand this world, well… it can be a bit overwhelming at best.

Let me state again that the purpose of the middle pillar exercise is to build energy through and around the aura and then circulate that energy. This creates a protective field around a person's aura and raises their vibration all at the same time. Additionally, it's a powerful method of bringing in God force energy. Because there are many versions of this, please feel free to do some research in order to find the version that will resonate most with you. The version printed in this book is a simplified version that uses only one of the Hebrew names of God. More complex versions require knowing and utilizing up to six different names.

Part One: Formation of the column of energy

Step One: Stand up straight, arms at the side. Close your eyes and take a few moments to contemplate how you feel physically, emotionally, and mentally. Take note on what the air feels like around you.

Step Two: Take 3 deep neutral breaths.

A neutral breath is a breath where a person breaths in through their nose deeply for a 3 or 6 count and then, without pause, exhales through their mouth for the same count as the inhalation breath. This type of breathing will almost always ground a person and help to restore their body to equilibrium.

Step Three: Visualize a ball of gold light above your head. Hold that image in your head. Take a deep breath and as you exhale chant "Yod Hey Vow Hey." Feel the gold light come down and engulf your head and radiate brightly.

Step Four: Visualize a ball of blue light around the chest and throat. Hold that image in your head. Take a deep breath and as you exhale chant again "Yod, Hey Vow Hey." Feel that blue light grow within your chest and throat and expand outward radiating brightly as it does so.

Step Five: Visualize a ball of yellow light around your stomach. Hold that image, take a deep breath in, and then exhale chanting "Yod Hey Vow Hey." Feel that yellow light expand outward and through you and radiate a pure yellow color.

Step Six: Visualize a ball of red light around your genitals. Hold that image, take a deep breath in, and then exhale chanting "Yod Hey Vow Hey." Feel that red light expand outward and glow a bright red.

Step Seven: Take a deep breath in and as you do so take the gold light from your head and, as you exhale, mentally bring it down around your throat and heart and combine it with the green. Again, inhale deeply, take the mixed color and, as you breathe out, bring it down to the stomach and mix it with the yellow. Take another deep breath and exhale as you mentally allow this mix to move down and mix with the red. With one more deep breath, take all of this and, as you exhale, bring it down and out through your feet into the earth below. As you focus on the energy at your feet moving into the earth again chant "Yod Hey Vow Hey."

Part Two: Circulation of the column of energy
Step Seven: Start a pattern of rhythmic breathing. Inhale for six, hold for three, and exhale for six. As you inhale take all this energy that is within the earth and bring it up the left side of your body and, when you exhale, bring it back down the right side. Mentally visualize the energy as it moves from the earth

and up the left side and back down through the right. Do this 5 to10 times or, if you are energy sensitive, until you feel the energy is circulating around you from left to right.

Step Eight: Now focusing on the earth again, take that central column of energy that you've grounded into the earth and bring it, like a tidal wave, up the back of your body, over your head, and down the front and back into an earth, forming a sphere around you. This too should be done to the 6-3-6 count. Repeat 5-10 times or again, if energy sensitive, until you feel the energy around you from back to front.

Part Three: Ending the Exercise

Step Nine: Take all the energy that is pooled into the earth below your feet and bring it up, visualizing each chakra and chakra color as you do so: red, orange, yellow, green, blue, indigo and purple. As you reach each new chakra point and color, take a deep breath and forcefully exhale to move the energy up the body. After you finish with the crown center, take one more deep breath and again forcefully exhale, shooting all this energy up and out through the top of your head into the universe.

Step Ten: Take a few moments to go sit down and just observe how you feel. If you need to, drink plenty of water. Contemplate what has happened during this exercise.

CHAPTER 7

Technique Four: Psychically Protecting the Aura

Now that we know how to strengthen the aura, are aware of the importance of proper thought and positive thinking, and know some actual physical means of protecting our energy, let's take a look at some of the psychic visualizations and additional actions that you can use to increase and strengthen your protection.

AROMATHERAPY

One cannot begin to express in words how important the sense of smell is to the human race. Smells, just like sounds, have a profound effect on our entire energy field. It takes just one scent to increase the energy in our aura or to trigger forgotten memories.

Who out there doesn't remember a favorite food that a beloved friend or relative use to make. A food whose scent you so strongly connect with that individual and time period of your life that immediately upon getting a whiff of it you are mentally transported back to either that person or that time period of your life.

Remember, everything is energy. The sense of smell is just another way we register energy. It is just another method that our human brain uses to make sense of a vibration. The energy associated with various scents can have a profound impact upon our health, aura, and healing.

There are many scents which will aid us in our psychic protections. I recommends, having the following essential oils and incenses available to you.

Oils

When it comes to oils, make sure you are selecting and using pure oils. Even though they don't normally come cheaply, they are well worth their price. Your oil collection should include at least the following:

Lavender: Lavender is a very important oil. It produces a very calming effect on the human body. It's known to reduce stress, lower the heart rate, and open the heart center. It is used both for relaxing and healing. It is great for sore muscles and relieving headaches. It is also said to aid in insomnia and nervous disorders. It is also a great aid for battling depression. Also, lavender is great at soothing burns!

In fact, aromatherapy was originally discovered by a French man. René-Maurice Gattefossé was mixing oils when he accidentally burned himself. In his agony he reached for the first liquid he could get a hold of and plunged his burnt hand into it.

By the next day, very little remnants of the burn remained. Curious as to exactly what he placed his hand into he went back to the lab and, upon careful research and retracing his steps, he found it to be lavender.

Frankincense: Said to help in treating inflammation and arthritis. It raises vibrations of a person or anything that it is applied to. It is also highly protective.

Eucalyptus: This oil is used for strengthening the body and preventing disease. It can revive someone who has fainted and is also an excellent treatment for lung problems, colds, and diabetes. Like Lavender oil, it also tends to produce a soothing and calming effect.

How do you use the oils? The simplest way is to add 2 to 3 drops to your bathwater at night. You can also put a few drops on your hands, rub them together, cup your hands under your nose, and then inhale. Likewise, you can add a drop or two to your hands and massage the soles of your feet with it. Finally, you can burn the oil in a diffuser. Please do not take any essential oils orally. They are not for internal use. Also, consider doing your own research on individual oils before using them. You always want to know what exactly a particular oil is meant for, and if there are any possible side effects that may be connected to using it.

INCENSES

Keep the following incenses available:

Rose: Rose is considered very special by many mystery schools. It is said that the scent of Rose will provide you with the power of invisibility, effectively cloaking your entire energy field. It is known as a healing scent and is said to create the energy that makes it possible for any of the mother goddess images (including Mother Mary) to be present.

Nag Champa: One of the oldest and most popular incenses in the world. It creates a tranquil and meditative environment, effectively allowing you to center and find your inner self/power.

Frankincense and Myrrh: Said to be gifts to baby Jesus. It is reported that many religions make use of these high vibratory and protective scents. The combination is especially great for cleansing, clearing, and protecting yourself and your environment.

Cedar: One of my personal favorites. Cedar incense is developed from the cedar tree and is a great scent to use for clearing and protecting. In addition, it gives one a feeling of being in touch with nature and of the healing powers of the natural world.

Desert Sage: Desert Sage is used for clearing an environment of 'negative vibes'. It also helps to create a meditative and sacred environment.

Indian Temple Incense: This sweet smelling incense is used primarily in Indian temples to create a pleasant, uplifting, yet relaxing environment. Next to Nag Champa, it tends to be one of the most popular incenses in the world.

White Sage: White Sage, like desert sage, can be used to clear an environment of 'negative vibes'. It is also great for sending away or banishing attachments or spiritual energies that you don't want around.

Now that it has been mentioned, this would be a good time to discuss spirit attachments and spirit possession.

First let's discuss spirit possession. A spirit possession is a rare thing to happen. In fact, of the innumerable times that I've been asked to investigate a possession or have had someone tell me that they knew someone who was possessed, I'm willing to guess that only about 1% of those cases *might* have been actually possessed.
A possession occurs when a spirit or 'demon' enters into the human body and takes control of it. The person loses all control and

becomes a host for the entity. Usually, if you look closely enough, you can still see some aspects of the person's former self somewhere within the physical body, but by far it becomes the property of the presence.

A spirit possession can only happen when a person invites the entity into them. This usually occurs by working with or using various dangerous psychic or magickal practices without proper knowledge and/or protective techniques being applied. By using these, you are in essence, consenting many times to allowing a spirit to come in.

Since this is the first time Demon's have been mentioned, I'd like to spend a few moments discussing them.

My personal belief is that demons are like angels. In other words, demons never have nor ever will be of the human race. Demons exist because of the nature of balance. For every act that occurs in our world an equal and opposite act or force must also exist. Whereas angels represents all that is "good" and structured, demons represent all that is "evil" and chaotic.

Thankfully, most people will never have the displeasure of dealing with real demons. Those who are intimately connected to the psychic, occult, metaphysical, and paranormal fields likely will come across such creatures at some point and time. You know what the old saying is…. "If you go looking for the Devil, the Devil's gonna come looken for you." The idea is similar. If you look for trouble, you can almost be certain that eventually you'll find trouble.

The protections in this book are aimed at keeping one safe even from these type of creatures. Even so, it isn't wise to go out looking for them in order to test what you are learning. When in doubt, always trust your intuition and play it safe.

Let's take the classic example of the Ouija board. I can't tell you the numerous problems I've seen occur as a result of using this psychic tool. It's unfortunate that the Ouija board is marketed as a toy, as this is where many of the problems arise. If people would use it as a serious tool and take the proper precautions prior to using it, there would be fewer dangers that occur due to the Ouija board. Ouija, the Most Dangerous Game, is a great book on this subject and it is highly recommended if you wish to learn more.

In any case, when a possession actually does occur there are only two ways to get the controlling entity out of the body. The first is via an exorcism within that person's chosen religious faith. If they have no religious faith, then the Roman Catholic exorcism is most complex (despite the fact that most Catholic Church officials re-fuse to acknowledge its existence. I know it does exist, as I've seen it myself in the basement of a church). To actually get a Roman Catholic priest to perform an exorcism is another story altogether. They must first gather proof that the possession is real and this can be a long process that involves not just the priest but medical and psychological professionals as well.

You should not attempt to perform an exorcism yourself unless you really know what you are doing and you are willing to take the risk of the entity leaping out from the host and entering your body. It takes a person with strong strength of will and a strong auric field to be able to do an exorcism properly.

Many exorcisms involve the use of holy water to drive the pos-sessing entity out and away. Whenever we use water with sea salt or kosher salt, we are making it a type of holy water. Holy water is created by the intent and the energy of the person who is blessing the water. Any person can make water holy provided the intention is pure. This also means that sea salt and kosher salt is very potent to clearing the human body. If you can get the possessed person to take a swim in the ocean, there is a good chance that they will be free of the possessing entity. The problem is, that entity usually will not allow the body to go anywhere near the ocean.

The other thing you can do, besides an exorcism, is to take the person to a psychological professional. This doctor, through the use of drugs, will sedate the host so much that the entity will be incapable of surviving within the structure as it now has no means of leeching energy off the host or anyone else.

A spirit attachment is different from a possession and is far more common. An attachment occurs when an entity literally attaches itself to someone and follows them around everywhere they go. An attachment differs from spirit guides in that spirit guides will not ever attempt to make decisions for you, and spirit guides are not seeking to take and use your energy.

To get rid of an attachment, the salt helps, but so does having the person work with the aura building exercises from before. The chakra visualization, in particular, is very important as it raises the vibration, making it more difficult for the attachment to hang on to that individual. You can also break attachments by using the cutting of psychic links exercise.

CUTTING PSYCHIC LINKS

We've talked about how links are created between people. We also mentioned how to physically cut and remove these links. In addition to doing this physically, you may also psychically cut and break links. The following exercise will help you to do this.

EXERCISE FOR CUTTING A SPECIFIC LINK

Close your eyes. Take 3 deep neutral breaths. In case you've forgot, a neutral breath is one where you inhale deeply through your nose for a 3 or 6 count and then immediately, without pause, exhale through your mouth for the same count.

Visualize the person with whom you want to break the link. See a tube of energy connecting you to them. Mentally, in your mind, call Archangel Michael to you. Ask Archangel Michael for help in breaking or cutting this link.

Please state to him if you want it temporarily cut or permanently cut. The author urges to use the permanent cutting very sparingly and only when you are sure you don't want anything to do with a person ever again. Let's face it, most of us, even when we are tired or angry, don't want to end a connection with someone permanently, we simply need a break from them.

After stating your intentions, feel yourself glowing with a bright gold light and then visualize Archangel Michael taking his sword and cutting through the tube (or tubes) of energy that are connecting you. Feel the aura where the tubes were connecting start to mend as the gold energy within fills the hole. Thank Archangel Michael.

This particular exercise is great to use before sleeping in order to temporarily cut away the day's ties to enable you to have deep and peaceful sleep. It can also be used, as has previously been mentioned, to cut away and rid yourself of entity attachments.

MIRRORS

Not real ones! We are talking about psychic mirrors. When you are in a situation where it feels as though you are being bombarded by energy, blasts, or downloads or you know you are getting into a possible situation where this may happen, take a few moments off, close your eyes and mentally put up mirrors around your body, the mirrors should be facing outward away from your body.

Mirrors are reflective. By placing the mirror reflecting outwards, you can ensure that if anything is projected or sent in your direction, it will be reflected and directed back to the sender. This is not considered black magick or anything like that. The reason is because the other person still has the ability or power to decide if they want to project such energy towards you.

For those of you who have a problem like claustrophobia or a fear of crowded public places, this is a great protective technique for you. The mirrors combined with the basic aura building exercise, if performed correctly before going out, will help you to function better in crowded public places for longer periods of time and without much anxiety or frustration.

You can give this a try before your next family reunion or public outing!

The Power of Prayer

Most people do not realize the importance of prayer or the power that it can bring to our lives. Prayer is a testimony of faith and devotion. Anything that I have suggested within the context of this book can be amplified by simply adding a prayer or some prayers to the end of the exercise, thought, or action.

Prayer is, literally, a direct link to the universal God force power. It puts into motion energies which are currently far beyond scientific or even human explanation.

Even so, within the pages of this book nothing is scientifically proven to work, except prayer! Funny isn't it? Science can't explain how it works, but science knows that it does work. There are many case studies of the miracles that have been performed because of the faith, devotion, and belief of prayer. These are medical miracles that have shocked the human world. Let's look at some of this scientific evidence.

- The August 31, 1998 issue of Jet Magazine asked the question: "Can praying lower high blood pressure?" Over 4,000 people over the age of 65 participated in this study. The study discovered that those who prayed and attended religious services had lower blood pressure than those who did not. Additionally, they discovered that the more religious and pious a person, the lower was their blood pressure.
- In the December 1998 issue of **Mc Call's Magazine** the question "How does prayer heal?" was focused upon. 1,902 twins were studied and it was learned that those who were committed to their spiritual lives had a lower chance of being depressed or suffering from an addiction like alcohol than those who did not. Additionally, those who were married and who engaged in prayer with their spouse had more stable marriages than those who did not.
- According to weird.com, in 1996, a double-blind pilot study at the UC San Francisco Medical Center was performed. All patients received standard care, but psychic healers prayed for 10 patients in the treatment group. The healers lived an average of 1,500 miles away from the patients. None of the patients knew which group they had been randomly assigned to, and thus did not know whether they were being prayed for or not. During the six-month study, four of the patients died - a typical mortality

rate. When the data was analyzed, the researchers learned that the four who had died were in the control group. All 10 who were prayed for were still alive. Also, the research results showed that the subjects who were not prayed for spent 600 percent more days in the hospital than those who were.

- Experiments in distance healing involving non-human subjects show that in a survey of 131 controlled experiments on spiritual healing, it was found that prayed-for rye grass grew taller, the prayed-for yeast resisted the toxic effects of cyanide, and the prayed-for test-tube bacteria grew faster.

Interesting what we keep discovering as we move into the future, isn't it?

The great thing about prayer is that it doesn't have to be elaborate. It doesn't even have to be ritualistic. In fact, the most effective prayers are not those which you learned from your parents or religious organizations but those that you have thought up and worded for yourself.

Catherine Ponder outlines a terrific method for creating your own prayers in her book **The Dynamic Laws of Prayer**.

I have outlined the steps below.

Creating your own Prayer

Step One: Begin by addressing your deity, be it God, a goddess, the universal life force, or your holy guardian angel.

Example: Oh great and loving God…

Step Two: Thank this deity for something that is important to you.

Example: I give you thanks for giving me the wisdom to write what others need.

Step Three: Make a plea for help.

Example: I beg you, oh wonderful God, grant me the resources and contacts to finish this project.

Step Four: State the reason for your plea.

Example: ...so that others are able to acquire this information which may change their lives for the better.

Step Five: Affirm that the plea has been answered already and thank your deity again.

Example: I know that through your name and power this is already done and I thank you for making it so from the depths of my spiritual soul.

Step Six: End with a word of affirmation. Amen, Blessed Be, Ah-Toe, etc.

Amen

So, our sample prayer when put together reads thus:

Oh great and loving God, I give you thanks for giving me the wisdom to write what others need. I beg you, oh wonderful God, grant me the resources and contacts to finish this project so that others are able to acquire this information which may change their lives for the better. I know that through your name and power this is already done and as such I thank you for making it so from the depth of my spiritual soul. Amen.

That was easy, wasn't it?! Now you have a formula with which you can design your own prayers so that you can directly communicate with the universal consciousness. Please note, however, that you must do more than just write down the words and say them. You must also fully believe and have faith in everything that you say.

GOLDEN VIBRATORY SHIELD OF POSITIVITY

If you remember we spoke of the importance of being positive and remaining positive back in technique one. You can greatly enhance your ability to remain positive by performing this exercise anytime you catch yourself having a negative thought.

Step One: Catch yourself having a negative thought or feeling in a negative mood.

Step Two: Close your eyes and take three deep breaths.

Step Three: Visualize yourself breathing in a golden light from the universe. Let that golden light flow throughout your entire body so that you are totally bathed in golden light.

Step Four: Feel that golden light shooting out all around you, pushing the negativity out at the same time.

Step Five: See that golden light create a large knight's shield. A shield that is as tall and as wide as you are. Feel this shield grow until you are surrounded on all sides by it.

Step Six: Feel this shield start to vibrate. Faster and faster. Watch it become a blur to human eyes. The faster it vibrates the more golden light shoots out around you.

Step Seven: Affirm *"I am surrounded by the golden light of positivity. Only positive and happy thoughts and moods are allowed within my presence. Only positive and happy thoughts and moods come from within me."*

I still remember the first time I used this powerful exercise. Upon finishing I felt light, airy, and as though I could take on the world. It was as though my whole being was buzzing! From time to time I forget about this important and special exercise; but I find myself constantly amazed every time I allow myself to go back to it and use it again. A feeling of renewed vigor once again returns to me and the air around me returns to being delightfully clear and clean. I strongly encourage people, both new and advanced, to make an effort at bringing this particular exercise into your daily life.

6. The Holy Breath of Calmness

This simple activity combines psychic protection and physical protection together. If you use it correctly and work with it often enough, you'll eventually be able to calm entire rooms and/or crowds that are angry, over emotional, and/or out of control.

Step One: Do whatever you need to do to put yourself into a calm state of being. This will not work if you have even a hint of doubt, fear, anxiety, or anger within your own being.

Step Two: Visualize yourself in the white light. Take a deep breath of the white light in, imagining that you are breathing that white light in through every pore of your physical body. Hold this white light energy inside of you.

Step Three: As you hold this white light energy inside of you imagine that you are one with your chosen higher power.

Imagine that you are filled entirely with calmness and visualize the most peaceful thing that you are capable of concentrating on.

Step Four: Cupping your hands over your mouth, forcefully push your cupped hands outward while exhaling sharply. As you do this imagine that the white light, now filled with the calmness of the higher power itself, filters into the room.

Step Five: Allow your breathing to return to normal and smile, fully believing in yourself and the higher power to be.

This works ten times better if you are a projective empath, but anyone is capable of producing a calm and tranquil environment by putting this exercise to good use.

Just in case you are wandering, a projective empath is someone that is capable of using their emotional energy to make/control how others feel. A receptive empath is when a person is capable of feeling and experiencing the same emotions that another is having.

As with all the exercises mentioned within this book, the more you use it, the stronger your ability, and competency with it, will become.

I usually tend to use this particular exercise when out in society and I find myself face to face with a person or people that seem to be hostile or irritable. Of course, common sense must be put to good use. You won't want to get right up in someone's face and blow this outward toward them; the repercussions may not be in your best interest. However, many times you can use this exercise from afar with great success.

The other time I tend to use this is when I'm around a rambunctious or crying child. The energy tends to be especially effective with babies because of their already inborn natural sensitivity that hasn't been fully shut down yet.

EMBRACE OF THE TREE SPIRIT

Our natural world around us is one of our most powerful friends and allies in our daily conscious and subconscious psychic battle. Plants, grass, water, and other natural elements all have a powerful, universal, and unconditionally loving aspect that are associated and connected to them. By tapping into this unconditional love we can both rid ourselves of negativity and replenish our life source energy. The exercise that follows is best done while sitting under a large tree with your back against it.

It is based off of a section from the well known book **The Celestine Prophecy.**

I encourage everyone to buy and read a copy of this book or, at the minimal, get a copy of the movie and watch it. There are so many great spiritual lessons and exercises that are part of the movie.

Step One: Take a comfortable position under the tree with your back to it. If no tree is available, take a comfortable position and imagine that you are sitting with your back against a large tree.

Step Two: Inhale deeply. Hold for a count of three. Exhale completely letting all the air exit your body. Repeat this two more times. Each time you exhale you should find yourself going deeper within yourself and forming a stronger and stronger connection with the tree.

Step Three: Feel the warmth and energy of the tree. Allow yourself to feel as though you are sitting beside a protective parental figure. Know that nothing can harm you while you are within this protective presence. Thank the tree for allowing you to share energy with it.

Step Four: Continue to breathe deeply and as you do this visualize all negativity that is around you or within you being absorbed by the tree. The tree is so protective that it escorts all such energy away from you and returns it back to the earth where it can be recycled, hopefully into something more vibrant and positive.

Step Five: When you find that you feel no more negativity in or around you, allow yourself to smile and feel a great sense of joy. Using this sense of joy, begin to visualize green and pink loving energy going from your heart center, out through your back, and into the tree. Visualize the tree absorbing this energy. Visualize the aura of the tree growing stronger. Feel the great sense of joy that comes with giving of yourself unconditionally to the earth.

Step Six: Now it's time to receive. Visualize and feel the energy from the tree, the same loving energy you sent to it, return to you three times as strong as that which you sent out. Feel this energy and watch it totally fill your body. As your body fills with this love visualize your aura becoming more vibrant, vibrating faster, and becoming more solid and strong. Feel and know that your aura is being infused with the love of the world itself. Watch it expand and feel yourself opening up with joy on all levels.

Step Seven: At this point you may repeat step five and six as many times as you desire. Allow yourself to freely experience the energy exchange. Each time you cycle through it, you will find that it feels more powerful and more expanded. When you are ready to conclude, thank the Tree and open your eyes and sit and contemplate on your experience for a few moments, before returning to your normal daily activities.

Gathering Your Spiritual Forces

There's nothing quite as spectacular as feeling yourself totally surrounded by your own personal army of protective forces and spirits.

Close your eyes. Sit back. Relax. Take a deep breath in. Hold it for a few moments. Exhale. Take another deep breath in. Hold it for a bit longer, than exhale again. Each time you breathe out you are going to feel yourself going deeper within yourself.

We are going to take a few moments to relax you completely. Visualize a screen in front of you. This screen is a magick screen that allows you to write on it. You are going to start writing the alphabet on that screen. Each time you finish a letter of the alphabet you will feel yourself becoming more and more relaxed, and going deeper and deeper into yourself. Begin now…

As you write the alphabet there is an understanding that any outside sounds that you hear will only cause you to go even deeper within. Nothing externally will interrupt you. In fact, it will only serve to help you achieve the best and deepest level of relaxation that you are capable of achieving.

Now that you are in a state of relaxation we need to be sure that nothing negative is with us. To do this, visualize a wishing well in front of you. Take a deep breath in and as you exhale see any and all fears, worries, and anxieties falling deep within that well. Good.

From your mind's eye, see yourself standing above this well. In a few moments we are going to count to three. When we reach three you will mentally jump into the well. When you do, you are going to instantly find yourself at a camp site. 1...2.....3.... Jump into the well and see yourself being transported to a camp site.

This camp site is your war room. It's your personal place to gather your own spiritual troops that are going to help advise you and protect you. Right now it is empty. It soon won't be though.

Walk over to a table. On this table there is a walkie-talkie. Through this walkie-talkie you can communicate to and request aid from anyone. Let's start gathering our troops by requesting the aid of a General.

Pick up your walkie-talkie and request to the universe that a General be sent to you to organize and lead the troops. When we count to three someone is going to appear next to you: this will be your General. 1...2.....3....

See the General. Who is it? Are they male or female? Old or young? Do you recognize them? What are they wearing? Know that this individual has been given permission by the universe to act in your best interest to help guard, guide, protect, and aid you in this moment of need and trouble.

Now, let's summon some angelic forces to work with our General. Let the General know you want angels working with you. Tell the General you grant and give permission for the angels to be a part of your life and to intervene in your life. When we count to three you are going to find those angels beginning to appear and form a protective circle around your camp. 1....2.....3....

Watch as the angels start to appear and one by one begin to make a protective wall and circle around the camp. Feel and know that you have angelic help with you in this time of need and trouble.

Now, we are going to let the General know that we want some archery units inside the camp. When we count to three you are going to see a group of soldiers enter into the camp and pick up bow and arrows. 1...2.....3

Watch the soldiers begin to enter the camp. See them as clearly as you can. Feel their presence.

At this point you can request whatever additional aid you think you need and the General and Universe will find a way to enlist its help. You may want a group of aliens with ray guns or something much more relaxed such as eagles that will scout for the rest of the army. Know that whatever you request, it will be there along with the general, the angelic forces, and the elemental forces.

When you are finished gathering your army, take a few moments to feel yourself surrounded by all this loving and protective energy. Know that you are strong, confident, and capable of dealing with whatever negative and troublesome concerns are occurring in your life. Know that, despite how things may seem, the universe is working in tandem with you to promote and allow for the best possible changes and results to take place within your life.

When you are finished count yourself back from 10 to 1. When you reach one you return to the normal waking state, fully aware of all that has occurred, and filled with a new found sense of contentment and preparedness.

Your Spiritual Armor

Many times we can avoid picking up negative vibrations and energy of people and locations through the process of equipping ourselves with our very own spiritual armor.

This particular exercise is very easy and requires only minimal concentration and visualizations.

Performing this exercise requires you to have a strong imagination or visualization ability and the faith to fully believe in what you're doing.

Start by physically pretending to put on a golden suit of armor. Imagine the breastplate being put into place. Imagine the leg armor being snapped on. Put on invisible gloves and bracelets. Slide on your invisible golden boots and lace them up. Pretend to put on your golden helmet and lock it into place.

Now, with your full suit of golden armor on, mentally see this armor radiate a bright blue light outward in every direction and then visualize white light raining down onto and around you.

Say a mental prayer or affirmation, showing gratitude and thanks that your protective armor has been given to you and is now on and in place.

You are now equipped with powerful armor which should prevent you from picking up negative energy, but still allow you to do whatever spiritual, healing, or psychic work that you need to do.

Elemental Circles

Elemental circles involve visualizing the self being in the middle of a circle that is surrounded by a particular elemental force. For example, you may want to be in an elemental circle of fire. You'd visualize fire springing up all around, burning bright, and feeling hot. Again, the more details you can add to your visualization, the stronger and more powerful it will be.

When would you use this? To understand that you first must understand the elemental representations.

- Fire: Physical and Passion
- Water: Emotions and Intuition
- Earth: Material and Foundation
- Air: Mental and Verbal
- Spirit: That which is beyond this world

With a little bit of creativity you can have an elemental circle to protect you from almost anything.

For psychic attacks (those that operate on an intuitional level here in the physical world), consider surrounding yourself with the air element. Why? Well, the intuition is noted as being part of the water element. Thus, the water element is "attacking" so to speak. To defeat, you surround yourself with the air element in order to "blow" the water (or attack) away from you.

Using this idea, you can surround yourself with a particular element and bring in those elemental qualities into your life.

Of course, some people enjoy layering their circle. So you could surround yourself with fire, water, earth, air and spirit all at once and have the complete elemental army assisting you. This, of course, is always best. It's also the one that takes the longest to visualize though. Each element has to be seen and felt clearly and vividly, and that will take you far longer than using just one particular elemental energy.

CHAPTER **8**

Technique Five: Magick Methods of Protection

Apart from the physical means of protection - proper thought, strengthening your aura, and psychic means of protecting your aura - it is also possible to work with magick to produce some outstandingly effective protection results.

But what is magick? Magick is the idea that by performing certain rituals or procedures and focusing intently upon them, you can create results here in the physical world. In other words, my own teacher once said to me: "The moment you realize that thought has the power to create, you are capable of working with magick."

A magick spell is the things you do or say which acts as a trigger to the subconscious mind to produce the effect that one intends and desires in the physical.

Magick is divided into three types: white magick, grey magick, and black magick. Black magick is any type of magick which has, or will have, an influence upon another person's free will. White magick is the opposite, anything that is done which does not influence another person's free will. Typically, White Magick is also thought of as protective magick. But be careful, protection magick, if not done properly, can end up easily becoming black magick, no matter how good the intent is.

Grey magick is the middle ground between white and black magick. Grey magick is any type of magick that is performed which may affect a person's free will, but won't necessarily.

Remember, the rule and law of magick, especially within Wiccan circles, is that whatever you put out will come back to you times three. This is referred to as the Law of Three. I say, whatever you put out will come back to you times ten. It may not happen right away, but sooner or later the universe must always rebalance itself. So think carefully before you attempt to perform magick on someone else: would you like something similar happening to you?

There are four magick spells below. These are all safe and come from the white magick approach.

Candle Power.

This is a very simple spell you can do.

You'll need a white candle, some aluminum foil, and a knife.

Step One: Begin by carving the name of the person whom you want to defend against or bind into the white candle. As you carve, make sure you place your intent into the candle that the person will have no further effect on you.

Step Two: Wrap the candle in the aluminum foil, shiny side facing in. This puts a protective shield, similar to the mirrors, around them. Only this time instead of reflecting negative energy away from you, it will reflect whatever they give out (to anyone) right back to them. This is a white magick approach as the person still has the free will to decide if they are going to put out the said energy when they are around you.

Step Three: Hold the candle in your right hand and send white light through the top of your head down through your arm and into the candle. As you do this, visualize the person not being able to come around you when they are in a negative mood or are throwing off negative energy.

Step Four: Put the wrapped candle into the freezer and leave it. Do not remove it until you are ready to break the spell. This action 'freezes' the person with the protective shield reflecting their own energy back to them and around them.

This is great, because not only will they be zapped by their own negative energy when they give it off, but when they choose to give off positive energy they will be zapped with that, making them feel better about themselves. Done properly, this spell can actually serve as a means of conditioning another person to having only positive thoughts and taking positive actions when around you.

Don't have a candle? Get an ice cube tray, write the name on a piece of paper, put it into the tray, fill it with water, and stick it in the freezer. This has the same effect as above. To break this spell, just melt the ice.

I can't even begin to tell you how powerful this simple little ritual is. It was originally taught to me by my own spiritual mentor when I had a nasty run in with a coven that was practicing black magick. Until then, I did not believe that such things could ever exist, could actually be done, or could have a negative impact on anyone's life.

Shortly after my run in with this group which shall remain nameless for the protection of others, my life started falling apart. Various members of the group would drop me notes and messages telling me how they were cursing me and so forth.

At first, I just laughed it off. My Rosicrucian studies had taught me that black or negative magick does not exist in the world if you don't believe in it. Here I was though, finding that things were just going from bad to worse.

I was in college at the time. My grades started dropping, I started getting nasty letters and emails from people I didn't even know, and bills that were normally low were skyrocketing to outlandish amounts.

Not knowing what to do, I finally broke down and wrote my own spiritual mentor and explained the situation to her. She told me it was probably about time that I started studying white protective high magick. She didn't have to mention it twice. By then, I was willing to do almost anything.

This was the very first spell I learned. Though it is by no means a part of what is considered high magick, it does work wonders. To make a long story short, after writing the coven's name on the candle and freezing it, they ceased all contact with me and my life actually returned to normal.

CHARGING A SYMBOL FOR PROTECTION

Pick your favorite amulet, charm, necklace, or bracelet.

Hold it in your right hand and see a stream of white/gold light coming down through you and into the object. As this energy moves into the object, verbally and clearly state the intent that you will be surrounded only by joy and happiness. Now, visualize the object being filled with blue and gold light and verbally and clearly state the intent that as long as you wear this, you will be protected from outside negative influences.

This, like the candle spell, seems so simple, and yet it has such amazing results. Most people will end up choosing their favorite holy symbol or some other symbol or piece of jewelry that is precious to them.

Once charged, all you have to do is carry it with you or wear it, and you'll reap the benefits of the protection you've magickally woven into the objects.

The Square of Saturn

A magick square is an energy that you copy onto a piece of paper which draws the effect of that energy into that paper. Then you can carry it around with you or you can build it into the house.

When working with any numerical square, you are evoking the numbers themselves. A number is a vibration and a symbol! One number is worth a thousand pictures!

Each magick square usually has a different technique associated with it. When you draw a square you should usually work with parchment paper, but you can also use copy or typing paper or any kind of paper.

The following technique was learned through one of my mentors.

Before you get started, make sure you clear the paper with salt and water and incense. White or Desert Sage is good for this. Air, earth, fire, and water should also be used in the clearing method.

Your paper should come into contact with all four elements. A simple way to do this is to being by sprinkling salt on the paper. Then wave it through the air. Next, hold it over a candle flame, being careful it doesn't catch fire. Finally, take a dab of water and touch it to the paper.

You can retrace everything below with a touch of your saliva to make it more powerful.

The Square of Saturn is usually used for protection. It can be made for other people and it can also be used to protect a house, car, person, or other place or thing.

Try to have 3, one for the house, one for the car, and one for yourself.

WHAT THE SQUARE OF SATURN LOOKS LIKE

4 9 2
3 5 7
8 1 6

On one side of the paper draw the person, place, or thing you want to protect.

Then think in your mind exactly how you want it to be protected.

Add to it some poetry, words, and symbols.

Such as:

Poem for protecting a home:

(Name of God, Goddess, Elemental, or Angel)
Bless this home
keep it safe from seen and unseen foes,
That all who enter here
bring only happiness, right help, and good cheer.

Words are very powerful as are names of angels, Gods, and deities. When using these over and over again, you are evoking and calling forth the power that has been used over the centuries. If you write your own poem, that is always better, but you can use poems written by others too, only make sure you understand what you are reading and what it means before evoking!

After you are done hold it in your right hand and breathe onto it.

Then turn it over and draw your grid, right to left, top to bottom. After you have finished drawing the grid start with number one and work your way around in numerical order filling in the numbers. As you draw each number concentrate and say either your poem or something like "Please God, Protect Me (or whoever or whatever) from all Negativity and Harm"

After you have done this turn it back over. Draw three crosses at the top of the paper. Once again top to bottom, right to left. Then draw three circles, starting with the outer circle, around it and going clockwise. This is for protection on all three planes - the physical, the emotional, and the intellectual or mental planes. As you draw the circles say your poem or words of protection again.

When you are finished recite your poem or words of protection one more time, holding it in your right hand and focusing your right eye on it. When you are done blow on it.

Now fold the papers either 4(foundation), 6(success), or if possible 8 (most powerful protection) times. Tie a red or purple string around it by wrapping it around the paper 4 times and tying 8 knots.

You now have a very powerful form of protection.

This, as with the first spell, was actually taught to me by my spiritual mentor. I don't know where she got it from, but I do know it can be found in many different sources with slight variations here and there.

Like the first spell, I've found that this actually works. One of my favorite activities is to make a square of Saturn for myself and carry it on me while traveling. I've discovered that by doing so I reduce by half the time I spend waiting in queues and going through security. Often, while carrying one on me, I have been able to walk right through security at airports and other places almost as though I was invisible. It also provides and produces a generally calm, secure, and safe feeling when carried.

CREATING AN EGG ELEMENTAL

Before we talk about how to create an egg elemental we first must understand what an elemental is.

There are basically three types of elementals within our world. The first is an actual elemental and is connected to one of the four elements (Earth, Air, Fire, Water). We've already worked with this type of elemental. The second type of elemental belongs to those creatures of the various core elemental spheres. For example, a water nymph is a type of elemental that hangs around water. A gnome or dwarf is an actual elemental that spends time around the earth elemental such as in a cavern or cave.

The last type of elemental is what we refer to as a created elemental and many times has nothing to do with one of the traditional four elementals. An example of such a created elemental would be an alcoholic elemental. Someone that is an alcoholic may accidently create an elemental that hangs around him/her constantly telling them that they really should have just one more drink. These created elementals usually have only one purpose and if they aren't getting their needs met (such as if the alcoholic they are linked to decides to stop drinking), they usually seek out someone that is capable of helping them to meet their needs.

These particular kinds of elementals can be destroyed. A technique taught by Donald Michael Kraig in his book **Modern Magick**, easily explains how to take care of these little guys. It can be found on page 124 and it is called the I.O.B. techniques which stands for… Identify, Objectify, and Banish.

The elementals that are connected to the four elements are most commonly thought of as fantasy creatures from fairy tales. This would include fairies, elves, gnomes, and so forth. A great deal of information can be found on these particular types of elementals in various books, especially those by Leadbetter, D.J. Conway, and Dion Fortune.

Our attention and focus is going to be on creating an elemental. These are also sometimes called elemental constructs. These normally come about in two different ways. The first, and what we are going to focus on, is by personal intent and applied will. The second way created or constructed elementals can arise is via repetitive thought. We will discuss how elementals are created and influence us via repetitive thought in the frequently asked questions section at the end of the book.

For now, I want to take the time to focus on how to make an egg elemental that will guard and protect your home from negative physical world and psychic invasions and/or attacks.

To create this little guy you will need a color marker, a raw egg, a candle, some incense, a bowl of dirt, and a small cup of water.

Step One: Light the candle and start burning your favorite type of incense. Dragon's Blood or Patchouli incense works great here, but any type of incense will be effective.

Step Two: Hold the egg in your right hand, close your eyes, and visualize white and gold light coming from above you, down through you and into the egg.

Step Three: Draw two eyes, a nose, a mouth, a pair of arms, and some feet on the egg with your marker. As you do this, be sure to give the to be egg elemental a name. Many cultures believe that to give a name to something is to give it power, and we are going to work with that concept here.

Step Four: Take the egg elemental and pass it over the candle flame saying *"By the element of fire I give you passion to form."* Then pass the egg elemental over the incense saying *"By the element of air your thoughts take form."* Now take some water and coat the egg saying *"The element of water gives you emotions that are true."* Now take some dirt and coat the egg with it uttering the words *"By the earth elemental your identity is finally through."* Then hold the egg elemental in your hand as you close your eyes and finish saying *"With my spirit also involved, you are created to heed my call. Protect this house from negativity of all kinds until permission is given to end your time."* This final part should be said while visualizing once again gold and white light energy flooding into the egg.

Step Five: At this point the elemental is basically created. We still have a few more things we need to do with it though. First, you should introduce yourself to it much like you would introduce yourself to any other person that you've met. After that introduction you need to remind the elemental that it was created for the purpose of working for you. Take it on a tour of your property, giving whatever instructions you want to give it for various rooms of the house. Kindness goes a long ways here. Be firm, yet loving and kind much in the same way as you would be with a child.

Step Six: After you've finished giving it a tour you will need to bury it outside in either the front or back yard, preferably where animals and other people will not find or discover it. Consider giving it some water or even food scraps from time to time to help promote good moral and fellowship. The water can be used as though you are watering a plant and the food scraps can be used as though you were using fertilizer. Kind words are also, as has been stated, very important.

After the egg elemental has been created it will take shape on the invisible planes and actually move around the parameter of your dwelling place acting as a guard. More than one pet of mine has been spooked by such a created elemental. It's helpful, as such, to introduce pets to your elemental and give instructions to both prior to burying it.

This is a very powerful form of protection. It's also your responsibility to destroy the created elemental should you ever need to move to another location. The easiest way to do that is through visualizing having a meeting with the elemental and telling it that you are releasing it from its services. Give your reason and then visualize the elemental transmuting form from the egg elemental into pure white or gold light and returning to the universal creative life force. Never release a created elemental to roam free into the world; it would be a huge injustice to both humanity and to the created elemental itself.

Why? Simply because elementals, when created in this fashion, must carry out the orders they are instructed to follow. Should you release a elemental from their post without destroying it, that elemental now has the ability to learn and grow on its own. This also means that it is no longer in service to you, and as such has a greater degree of freedom over how they interact with other life forms.

While that may sound great at first, sooner or later trouble is bound to be found. Best to avoid such trouble at all cost so you don't have to use your precious time and energy to correct what shouldn't have fallen by the wayside in the first place.

CHAPTER 9

Technique Six: Protecting Others

Finally, besides knowing how to protect, no psychic self defense book would be complete without a section devoted to the ever important procedure of cleansing and clearing.

House/Work/Car

Keeping your house and work space clear are of utmost importance. Think about it. You spend the majority of your life in these places. If they aren't clear of negative vibrations you are bound to pick them up sooner or later. Clearings should happen at least four times a year at each of the solstices and equinoxes. However, some people may want to do it more often. This is going to be especially true if there are a lot of negative emotions that tend to come into your space or that your space seems to create.

As a good example, how many reading this have ever been in a fight or an argument with someone? When this fight or argument takes place, that energy is being produced in whatever room you're having the fight/argument in. You may both leave the room, but the moment someone else comes into that room it is very likely that they will suddenly feel as though they need to start or be involved in a fight. Why? It is because they are walking right back into the same energy that was left there. Can you now see the importance of keeping your space and environment cleared?

To clear your house, work space, or even your car, do the following:

Step One: Get some sage, kosher or sea salt, and a spray bottle.

As you will recall, sage is a very powerful cleansing and clearing agent and something that the Native Americans of old swear by. If you don't have sage available try using frankincense or cedar wood incense. Both of these are also awesome clearing agents.

Step Two: Dilute the kosher or sea salt in a spray bottle filled with water. It doesn't take a whole lot! At most, all that is required is two pinches of the salt. The reason you should use kosher or sea salt is because they are pure salts. When added to water and sprayed into the air this creates an actual chemical reaction (positive and negative ions colliding with each other) that will not only clear on a psychic level, but will actually leave the room light and airy.

Step Three: Before you start, open a window or a door if possible, to allow positive energy to come in and negative energy to go out.

Starting in the easternmost corner of the space and working around clockwise from bottom to top, begin to burn the sage and carry it from corner to corner. We say start in the east because that is the location of the rising sun and the direction that many, over the years, have assigned as holding the most power. If you don't know which way east is, don't fret. Create in your mind a momentarily geographical east and begin there. As long as you believe you are working clockwise starting in the east, your clearing will be just as effective as if you actually started in the east.

Step Four: As you carry the sage from corner to corner say a little prayer. Something simple is fine.

"Allow only positive energy to be present here, take negativity away from here."

The author enjoys using the prayer of St. Michael the Archangel.

"Michael the Archangel, defend us in our daily battles. Be our safeguard against the wickedness and snarls of the devil. Rebuke him, we humbly pray, and do thou, oh prince of the heavenly hosts, by the power of God, cast into hell Satan and all evil spirits who wander the world seeking to ruin the souls of man here on earth."

Step Five: Now, using the spray bottle and water, go back through each room spraying a mist of the sea/kosher salt water into the air.

Step Six: Make your way to every window and door and make either a banishing pentagram or banishing cross in the air above the entryway to seal out negative energy.

Step Seven: Go through each room and visually see yourself collecting in your hands any leftover negativity that may be present. Return to the open window, visualize yourself tossing the negative energy out, then close the window and once again draw either a banishing cross or pentagram over the window.

Still not feeling right? Try setting a glass or cup of water with sea or kosher salt in one corner of the room. Negativity will be drawn into it. Just make sure you flush it every night before bed. You can create a similar effect by putting a small amount of sea or kosher salt in a cup or jar and placing it somewhere inside the room. This is usually good for about 30 days before you'll need to toss it out to mother earth and replenish the cup. Amethyst can also be placed around your space - it has an effect of raising vibration and protecting.

CLEANSING/PROTECTING OTHERS

The best way to cleanse another person is to use sage and trace an outline around their body while visualizing white light filling in the outside of the aura. Then you go back and move from bottom to top working your way through each of the chakras, visualizing a gold light filling each of them.

Protecting another person is also an easy task. When you do any of the exercises from this book, you have the option of either holding the person's hand that you want to protect, or visualizing them as standing right next to you. Doing either of these two things while you perform the protection ritual or exercises will ensure that they are included within your protections.

I have known many of my students who were parents that have found it extremely helpful to hold their child or be close to their child while doing some of the exercises in this book. By doing so, they are helping to promote a healthy lifestyle, energy, and protective field around them. Later in life, that child will be capable of keeping their own aura and energy strong and healthy because they've already had previous experience and exposure through a trusted parental figure.

Frequently Asked Questions

The questions that follow are frequently asked when it comes to psychic self defense and energy awareness. There are many variations to these questions with which many in the field have probably already answered, but here is my personal take on them.

1. **As long as I have my faith, I am fully protected, right? Then why would I need to do any of these things in this book? I am a strong (insert religion) follower.**

This question is a tricky one, but we will try to discuss it to the best of our ability. This is both true and false at the same time.

In the ideal world, in the ideal human one has what we shall term true faith. True faith is an unwavering understanding and knowledge in a power far above and beyond what we are capable of understanding on the human level and a total trust in that power. When one has true faith, no doubt or hesitation, and total trust in that higher power, then yes.... they are pretty much fully protected because their vibration level is usually much quicker than the average person within our world. For the vast majority of us, including the author of this work, true faith is not something we have had, do have, or ever will have. Though many of us would like to proclaim with certitude that we have that level of faith and trust in divinity, the truth is that most of us have at least some speck of doubt somewhere within the conscious or unconscious part of our mind. As such, most of us would like to think that if we just rattle off a prayer to the divine source of all that, everything will be ok. This would be quite misleading, though. Remember the old saying "God helps those who help themselves"?

As such, it's important to understand that the majority of us, even though we have a strong religious or spiritual background and much faith connected to that background, we would do well to make use of the techniques that have been outlined and presented to you throughout this book. Thus, we have the double protection of both a universal god force as well as personal protections that we are employing to "help ourselves."

2.   I developed protections in a past life where nothing could harm me or stop me. As such I feel very safe here in the present. Do you think this is possible?

I'm a firm believer that almost anything is possible. This does not fall into that realm of almost anything. Those who put their ego first are the ones who tend to be in the most danger of being harmed by these energy attacks that take place every day. Besides, the past is not the present.

Questions 1 and 2 have much in common and if you consider the reply to question 1 you can easily apply the concepts to question 2. For your own good, working with and practicing the techniques outlined in this book will be of great benefit to you.

3. My guides are very important to me. I am a firm believer that I must do everything they tell me to. What are your thoughts on this?

In order to answer this question we first must have an understanding on what guides are and what they are not.

The vast majority of guides lived life as human beings or lived a physical human existence at some point in time. In fact, most guides have lived multiple human lives and incarnations. As such, they tend to bring with them a great deal of experience about our world and the nature of humanity. However, please also keep in mind that guides are not infallible spiritual energies. Most guides who are assigned to us or that we choose are working in cooperation with us. Yes, we are learning various things from them, but at the same time they are learning several things from us. For example, my protector guide Alexander was a Roman warrior. In fact, he was pretty much undefeated in his battling years. Alexander has a temper and is a foul mouth. His solution to most things is "kick their ass." Well, even I know that this type of action is not always (nor is usually) the best course of action to take. He's learning from me patience and the need to look at things from a different point of view. At the same time, I don't tend to be the most aggressive person in the world and for a very long time I had the problem of letting people walk over me and treating me as a doormat. Alexander, as one of my guides, has done a magnificent job of teaching and helping me to learn that I don't have to allow others to treat me that way and that, in fact people respect you more when you have a healthy sense of respect for yourself.

The point that's being made here is that guides are not perfect just as we are not perfect. We, as a human race, tend to want to place our responsibility on anyone or anything other than ourselves. Yet, when we learn that we are responsible for all things that happen to us, no matter how good or bad they feel, and know that we have the ability and power to control and alter these things, only then are we learning to access the God force which lies within. To place responsibility on another person is considered to be in bad taste, so why would it be any different to place responsibility on a guide - someone who is coexisting with us as our closest friend and ally? No, they won't take responsibility for the things we choose to do with our free will and they shouldn't. They will have their suggestions about what we should or shouldn't do and that will be from their own perspective and their own opinion. Even though they usually known what is best for us and what's most likely going to help us grow, we still ultimately have the free will to follow them or to go out on our own and do our own thing. Sometimes it's better to go our own route. Other times it isn't. That's what this human life is all about - learning from every action that we take and every reaction that follows.

So, use your common sense and be willing to listen to your guides, but don't make the mistake of following them blindly just because you believe they should know all.

4. **I've never really made an attempt at improving my living circumstances. I'm not dirt poor, but I don't have much wealth either. I feel like I'm constantly struggling, yet I think that this is what the universe wants of me. What do you think?**

I think you are missing the point of this human life. The video *The Secret* has done a great service to humanity by helping people to see things from a totally different perspective. At one point in the not too distant past it was believed that in order to be a spiritual person you had to deny the existence of the material world. That couldn't be further from the truth! In fact, you can't possibly be at your best spiritually or any other way if you ignore the physical reality into which you have been incarnated.

We are meant to have whatever it is we desire - happiness, sadness, anger, moodiness, riches, poverty, anything that we want the universe will give us. As *The Secret* tells us, most of us focus on the things we don't want and then we refuse to accept and take on responsibility for the things that happen. This puts us in a very bad place on both an emotional and mental level and makes it hard to recover. Only when we accept responsibility for the way our life is, both the good and bad, and truly put our heart and soul into focusing on and seeking the things that we want, that make us feel good, will we be able to truly connect to the greatest aspects of the spiritual world.

Spirituality is about doing the best for ourselves so that we can help others locate, find, and do the best for themselves on a spiritual level. Do yourself a favor, take the time to realize that you can be both rich and wealthy on all levels AND spiritual too, and that they go hand in hand, and do not work against each other.

5. Do ghosts/spirits harm other people? Will I get possessed?

In order to answer this question we must separate out four aspects of the unseen world. There are ghosts, there are apparitions, there are spirits, and there are poltergeists.

Ghosts: Ghosts are spiritual presences that, through the use of energy, usually take on a physical form in order to interact with the physical environment. Most ghosts are not evil or bad, rather they are spiritual energies that have a message which they need to get across to someone. Many ghosts do not, in fact, even know that they are ghosts and as such simply helping them to understand this is all that is needed for them to move on.

Apparitions: An apparition isn't really a ghost at all! It's more like a memory that, because of the intense emotions and circumstances surrounding it, has been locked into time and place. Thus, when you encounter an apparition interacting with it does little to no good, because nothing is really there except for the memory.

For instance, let us suppose that a man and his wife are having an argument. The man takes out a gun and shoots his wife then turns the gun on himself. Many years later, people start to notice that there is a man with a gun and they hear the shrieking of a woman and this centers around one room of this home. What we have here is not ghosts, but rather apparitions. The memory of the event is firmly trapped inside that particular room and when a certain amount of energy or a certain type of energy is present; that energy sets off that memory so that it plays out, like someone accidentally touching the Start button on a VCR which starts playing whatever tape is in the machine.

The best way to end apparitions is via a good clearing and cleansing of the area. See clearings earlier in the book for more information.

Spirits: A spirit, unlike a ghost, usually does not take on a physical form, but exists around a person in a purely energetic form which is often only visible to someone with clairvoyance. Most spirits choose to interact with our world, to hang around loved ones, and to check on us. Sometimes, like a ghost, they may not be aware that they have crossed over. It is usually spirits that a medium connects with.

Poltergeist: A Poltergeist, a word which means noisy ghost, is most often associated with the things that people are truly frightened of. Examples of poltergeist activity include chairs moving or pictures spinning. The thing about Poltergeists is that they develop due to all the energy that is in the environment. Most often, we see cases of poltergeist activity in homes that have children who are just entering their teens. All that pent up sexual energy and all the changing hormones produce energy that is often uncontrolled.

Uncontrolled energy is still energy and so what happens is that the uncontrolled energy ends up making pictures spin and things move. When these children in early teens learn to control their emotions and energy the so called poltergeists stop being active.

The same can be true in any environment which contains a lot of high stress or high sexual energy. When this energy is not properly grounded it can create results here in the physical world.

What this basically means is that for an estimated 95% of the population that experiences ghosts, apparitions, spirits, or poltergeists, there is no chance of any real harm coming to them.

Every now and again, on rare occasions, we do encounter in our physical world something of a darker type of energy that is altogether evil at its very core. These energies usually are not coming from any of the above, but rather are connected to some type of demonic energy that has been allowed into our world. Please understand the following about such energies. These energies, the majority of the time, can only hurt you if you allow them to. Likewise, it is not possible for a person to be possessed by such energy unless that particular person meddles with psychic stuff which they don't understand or which they subconsciously want and therefore allow to happen.

When a case of true possession happens there is usually one of two routes that someone can go in order to get rid of the entity.

First, they can do a good old-fashioned exorcism. This will usually only work when people have some background or connection with a religion or a religious belief. At the very least, belief in God or a universal God force needs to be present by the one performing the exorcism. There are many types of exorcisms. The Roman Catholic Rite of the Exorcism is perhaps the most popular and the one most often glamorized by Hollywood. Every religion has its own form of an exorcism ritual.

The second thing one can do is to see a counselor or psychiatrist in which case through the use of drugs and repetitive mental correction, the said force either becomes dormant within the body or is driven out altogether because they can no longer tolerate being within the energy field.

Attachments are much more common than actual possessions. An attachment is a spiritual energy or entity that is attached to you or vice versa. Attachments can form at almost any time, but are most often seen when a relative that we were very close to crosses over and either we or they aren't ready for the crossing to happen. Understand, not all attachments are bad. They are only considered bad if they end up interfering in a person's life or if they make an attempt to take over or control that person's life. Thus, just because Aunt Betty wants you to continue giving money to her children long after she has passed away doesn't mean you are obliged to do so.

There are various methods for ending or breaking attachments. The more common ones would be any of the methods that you read about in the prior section of the book dealing with cleaning and clearing methods.

6. **In your prayer section you talk about designing and creating your own prayers. What if for instance, I really like Hail Mary? Does this mean I shouldn't say it?**

Not at all! Prayer is a personal thing. It's about you communicating with your deity. As long as you put a lot of energy, faith, and belief into prayers already designed or given to you by others, you can recite any prayer! There truly is no right or wrong way to pray. What is important is fostering that spiritual connection which will, in turn, aid not only your spiritual and psychic protection, but will help you come into a holistic balance of the physical, emotional, mental, intuitive, and spiritual.

7.   Can you tell us a little more on aura and traumatic events? Do these have an effect on the aura? Does our aura effect how traumatic a traumatic event will be?

Every person will end up with holes in their aura when they go through a traumatic event. The stronger the aura is initially before the event, and the frame of mind with which the person approaches the traumatic event will determine how big and how many holes end up in the aura, as well as ultimately how much energy is lost during those times.

A person who can take a traumatic event and find some good in it, no matter how small, will always end up repairing their aura faster than people who focus on things from victim mentality.

When we have others to share our traumatic moments with, when we are freely given the support of their aura and energy, we tend to heal and repair our own aura much faster. Please note that this is not the same as dumping. When we really do want to be helped and are willing to listen, take direction, and attempt to make changes in our life for the better, we don't dump. It's when we don't really care about what the other person says and only want to get things out of our system without any intention of fixing the problem that we end up dumping.

8. What happens when people cooperate or do things to- gether on a project? This is obviously two energies that are working together. How does that work?

When two or more people combine their efforts, they are in es- sence, pooling their energy, and their auras are coming together. This is the reason many psychic protection classes and books warn of the dangerous of committing yourself to a group, especially a magickal one like a coven or esoteric organization.

It's easy to see such dangers. Think about it. When you look at any group dynamic there is a certain feel or energy to it. Remove just one person from that group or add just one person and the entire feel and energy of that group changes! In groups, especial- ly magick groups, we are linking our energy fields very strongly to each other. It's almost as if we freely choose to open that door in the shield and allow our energies to mix freely. The problem with this is that if the group isn't capable of being cohesive, or if you have just one bad apple in the group, there is a big probability that the whole group could suffer.

The moral here is: know what you're getting yourself involved in should you ever decide to join a group of any type. Moreover, if for some reason you don't feel comfortable, make sure you leave the group.

This same dynamic also helps to explain how we are capable of lending our aura energy to another person in order to protect and/or support them. A good example of this would be an argu- ment that two people are having. Let's suppose that two women are having a heated argument. One of them exhausts her en- ergy and is now tired, and about to break down. A third person, who just happens to be listening to this argument, steps in and supports or backs up the woman who is now tired. Suddenly, this tired woman gets what appears to be a second wind, and 'comes back' now more confident and stronger than before. The individual that was originally winning the argument is now forced to back down.

What happened? This third person, by joining forces with the tired woman, created a combined aura between the two of them. This enabled the tired woman to quickly restore lost energy and it also caused the two of them to have a stronger and more powerful aura than just one person.

9. **You spoke earlier of how created elementals or elemental constructs can be created via repetitive thought and how more needs to be discussed on that later. Would you please share your thoughts on this?**

We know that what we think about must be created or come into being. Every thought we have, especially those powered by emotions, will take form in either the physical world or the invisible world that is termed the astral.

Sometimes these thoughts create a little creature, an elemental if you will, that becomes infused with power to follow one particular thought and to attempt to persuade you into continuing a said pattern or engaging in a said behavior.

The most common way to see and understand this is by thinking of an alcoholic or anyone that has a severe addiction. The person with the addiction, by thinking about that which they are addicted to strongly enough and with enough emotion, creates an elemental that feeds off this emotion.

Thus, the alcoholic, for example, may create by accidental thought, a little creature that will attach itself to him and constantly tell him over and over *"It's ok, you can have just one more drink."* By feeding into what the elemental wants he continues to supply it with power and thus makes it more real and stronger by each passing drink.

These particular types of elementals need to be destroyed by the person who created them and this can only happen when they are conscious of what is happening and then actively choose to take control over their life and emotions. A great visualization that can help them with this is by invoking the archangel Michael and seeing Michael take the said elemental and suck it into a vacuum from which it can't escape. The other common visualization that can be used to get rid of these type of elementals (or negative thoughts) is to see the elemental or negative thought and then visualize yourself holding a magick wand which can make things shrink. Point the wand at the creature/thought and watch it shrink and shrink until nothing remains. This same technique is wonderful to use when you catch yourself having a negative thought and want to get rid of it so that you can replace it with a more positively charged thought.

10. Just curious, but what if you don't believe in God? If I am an Atheist does this mean that your stuff won't work for me?

I'm going to argue that even the strictest Atheist has a belief in God. Just not in the form that most people think of.

The nature of Atheism is to believe in nothing. Most Atheists, as such, create a very strong internal belief in themselves. They don't put their power in a higher power, rather they put their power in themselves and their own hands.

Many religions have a very strong belief that a part of the universal energy or a part of God is within each of us.

For someone like me, who holds that belief, it's easy to see how an Atheist, a person that believes in no higher power but who still has a deep rooted belief in themselves and that are capable of controlling their own lives... From my perspective, this belief in the self is equal to the belief in God simply because that energy is within every person.

The biggest problem with the New Age field that I've encountered is the terminology. Everyone wants to have the next "big" thing or wants to be "special." The truth is, we are ALL special equally. Be a person believe in a God or not, as long as they believe in themselves they are tapping into that powerful energy which, from my belief system, comes from that power known by man as God.

11. You tend to talk a lot about angels, especially when performing the LBRP... what if I don't believe in Angels? Am I not able to do this exercise?

It's interesting, but a very large portion of the world does believe in angels. Angels almost transcend religion all together. In fact, almost every religion has their form and version of the angelic race.

However, the LBRP can be performed without the angel visualization. Wicca does something similar when they are casting their circle. Shamanism, likewise, also perform a similar ritual in cleansing and protecting an area. Neither of these two groups usually give a lot of attention, if any, to angelic energy.

What they do give attention to is directional energy.

Each angel that was mentioned correspondence to a natural direction. The angel and the direction have similar energy.

East = Raphael = Air energy
South = Michael = Fire energy
West = Gabriel = Water energy
North = Uriel = Earth energy

If you don't believe in the angels just substitute the element energy connected to the direction and angel. For example you could say "before me air", "behind me water", "on my right side fire", and "on my left side earth"........

I do encourage you to try it both ways and see which one feels best to you. Likewise, there are Latin and Greek versions of the LBRP that are available. Consider trying a different language and seeing if you resonate more with it.

We use Hebrew in this book, again, because that was the way I was originally taught.

Acknowledgements

There are so many people currently in my life that I'm grateful to. Basically, if I know you, I appreciate and value you on some level. There are, however, a few people and organizations that deserve extra special mention.

Thomas Moore: You are truly one of the best and greatest friends anyone could ever ask for. Anyone that knows you should feel extra blessed that you are apart of their life. You have been by my side through the hardest of time and have always helped me to continue to hold my head high. You are a talented reader and you have a phenomenal amount of knowledge to share with others. Http://inperfectloveinperfecttrust.webs.com

Chris Demint , Dawn Carroll, Chuck Millar, and Rick and Shelly Jenkins: You are all very special friends to me and I feel especially grateful that I have you in my life. I miss gaming with all of you, and hopefully in the future some of us can get together and do some dungeons and dragons gaming.

Justin Arnold: A very big special thanks goes to you my friend from afar. You're talent and ability has helped me to both organize and edit this book. I will highly recommend you to everyone for their writing and/or editor needs. www.the**mightierpen**.co.uk/

Gerald O'Donnell , Sandy Anastasi, John Maerz, Christy Ottinger, Jason Oliver, Terrance Shueman, and Stacey Toma: Teachers are the people that make the biggest difference in our lives. It is because of our teachers that we become better people and learn the skills, wisdom, and knowledge to tackle the world. I feel very blessed and honored to consider each of you a teacher of mine. No matter what differences you may have had with each other in the past, present, or future, your combined efforts have enhanced my growth and made me the person I am today and that I continue to develop into.

Rosicrucian AMORC and Masons: Two affiliations that have taught me much about both being a better man and living a spiritual life to the fullest.

My Family: Mom, grandpa (James Potter) and everyone else past, present, and future. Though we may not talk much, there is still a deep aspect of myself that is thankful and grateful for the love, kindness, and wisdom that you've shared with me over the years.

I also want to thank all my clients and students - past, present, and future. I learn as much from them as they learn from me.

Finally, and most importantly,
God: It is in God or that great universal spiritual cosmic consciousness which is the architect of the universe that truly all things are possible.

Bibliography

Anastasi, Sandy. Applied Magick. AIIS. 1993.

Anastasi, Sandy. Psychic Development 1: The fundamentals. AIIS. 2003.

Anastasi, Sandy. Psychic Self Defense. AIIS, 1993.

Andrews, Ted. Psychic Protection. Dragonhawk Publishing, 1998.

Assaraf, John & Smith, Murray. The Answer. Atria Books, 2008.

Byrne, Rhonda. The Secret. Atria Books/Beyond Words, 2006.

Denning, Melita and Osborne Phillips. The Llewellyn Practical Guide To Psychic Self-Defense & Well Being. Llewellyn Publications, 2nd edition, 1983.

Fortune, Dione. Psychic Self-Defense. Weiser Books; Revised edition, 2001.

Hall, Judy. The Art of Psychic Protection. Weiser Books, 1997.

Hill, Napoleon. Think and Grow Rich. JMW Group, Inc, 2005.

Hunt, Stoker. Ouija: The Most Dangerous Game. Harper Paperbacks, 1992.

Kraig, Donald Michael. Modern Magick. Llewellyn Publications, 2nd edition, 1988.

Mickaharic, Draia. Spiritual Cleansing: Handbook of Psychic Protection. Weiser Books, 21 Anv edition, 2003.

Ponder, Catherine. The Dynamic Laws of Prayer. De Vorss & Company, 1987

Redfield, James. The Celestine Prophecy. Warner Books, 1993.

Robbins, Anthony. Unlimited Power. Simon & Schuster, 1986.

Wattles, Wallace. The Science of Getting Rich. 1912.

Index

CPSIA information can be obtained at www.ICGtesting.com
Printed in the USA
LVOW112236010412

275693LV00009B/88/P